Great Modern Composers

GREAT MODERN COMPOSERS

BY

DANIEL GREGORY MASON

BIOGRAPHICAL SECTIONS BY MARY L. MASON

Essay Index Reprint Series

BOOKS FOR LIBRARIES PRESS
FREEPORT, NEW YORK

First Published 1916
Reprinted 1968

Originally published as Volume II in
THE APPRECIATION OF MUSIC

LIBRARY OF CONGRESS CATALOG CARD NUMBER:
68-20319

PRINTED IN THE UNITED STATES OF AMERICA

CONTENTS

PREFATORY NOTE

HIS book is intended as a sequel to "The Appreciation of Music," written some years ago by the present writer in collaboration with Mr. Thomas Whitney Surette. That volume carried the study of music from early times up to the death of Beethoven (1827); the present one takes it up there and carries it through the most important of the Romantic Composers and the composers of program music down to the present day, ending with studies of the two most widely accepted living musicians, Strauss and Debussy.

The method of study which has secured so gratifying a reception for "The Appreciation of Music" has been retained here. The composers are discussed from the point of view of the listener; their chief qualities are pointed out as they may be noticed by an attentive layman; and only the rendition and interpretation of the examples for analysis require technical skill. Wherever the book is used as a text in schools, colleges or clubs, the teacher or leader should play and discuss these examples with great minuteness, as they are invaluable in bringing to a definite focus the more general discussion. Those private readers who cannot play them, however, may still get a helpful notion of their bearing by reading the descriptive notes, even without the music.

During the past few years the study of the appreciation of music has passed the experimental stage and taken rank as an accepted part of a liberal education. Signs are not wanting that it is already affecting beneficially the standards of musical taste current among us. In the measure that it can do so, it will inevitably contribute not only to the reception, but to the production, of good music by Americans. It is the author's hope that this book may contribute its mite toward this ever to be desired end.

D. G. M.

New York, January 1, 1916.

I

CHAPTER I

Romanticism and Realism in Music

I

IN OUR study of the development of music from the primitive folk-song up to the symphony of Beethoven* we have become acquainted once for all with the fundamental principles of instrumental music, and with the chief types of structure to which it conforms, and which it is necessary for the music-lover to understand in order to listen to it intelligently. We have seen how its "motives" and themes grow into complete pieces through processes of development as spontaneous, as inevitable, as those of any other organic life, such as that of plants or animals. We have analyzed the standard types of organization which thus resulted in the course of the classic period: the folk-song, the brief two- or three-part dances of the old suite, the minuet, the theme and variations, the rondo, and, most complex of all, the sonata-form, which plays so vital a part in all sonatas, quartets, over-

Retrospective.

*"The Appreciation of Music."

tures, and symphonies. In the further study now before us we shall encounter many novel applications of these principles and forms, but nothing that is absolutely new. The foundations of an art are, like those of a science, unchangeable because derived from permanent truth; it is surfaces, rather than essences, that change; and a Richard Strauss can no more get on without expounding, developing, and restating themes, than an automobile or an aeroplane can defy the laws of gravity.

The essential qualities of music do not change.

It is well to insist at the outset on this continuity of the whole history of music, because otherwise the widespread fallacy that "romantic" and "programme" music essentially differ from the music of the classic period might seem to be supported by the emphasis on the differences between them that we shall have to make when we come to analyze them at close quarters. The differences are in reality far less important than the underlying likeness. Whether a piece of music has or has not a specific title, whether it has or has not a detailed programme, whether it is written for a large or a small body of players—all such considerations are trivial enough compared with the questions, which we ask of all music irrespective of its date or school: "Is it beautiful?" "Is it expressive?" "Is it individual?" "Has it interesting ideas, clearly arranged and logically developed?" Whenever the answers are in the affirmative it will be found that the music, whatever its modernity, is music in the old sense. Often its use of the ancient methods will be found almost surprisingly naïve. Chopin's "Raindrop" Prelude owes its eerie charm to a most poetic application of the device the old fugue composers used to call a "pedal point." In the first movement of César Franck's Symphony, one of the noblest passages is the "canon" he makes of his chief theme at its recapitulation. The wittiest symphonic poem of the impish Dr. Richard Strauss, "Till Eulenspiegel's Merry Pranks," as he himself informs us on the title-page, is "in rondo form"; and, what is more, its humor is due to precisely the kind of effects used with the same intent by Beethoven.

II

What is Romanticism?

In applying the term "romanticism" to the music of the early nineteenth century, then, and in referring to the composers who immediately followed Beethoven, notably Schubert, Schumann, Mendelssohn, and Chopin, as the "romantic composers," we do not intend to make a sharp demarcation between two essentially different arts, but rather to indicate a gradual shifting in the emphasis placed upon the various elements, none of which is altogether absent from the music of any period. Romanticism tends to make expression as individual, as special, and as vivid as possible; it aims at the particular rather than the general, cultivating the lyric style for the expression of the particular person and building upon the folk-song for the expression of the particular nation or race. It tends to neglect the wider development of thought in which classicism especially rejoices, and is somewhat indifferent to proportion, balance, comprehensive arrangement—to all that we may call the monumental side of art. It takes great interest in the sensuous charm of its material (in the case of music, sound) and spares no effort to refine and diversify the sensuous effects at its disposal. In its extreme phases it demands an increasing literalness in expression, until it may pass over, as in what is known as "programme music," from romanticism properly so called into realism.

III

Special expression.

Undoubtedly the most constant of all the marks of romanticism is the tendency to specialize expression. The wide general types of human feeling, joy and sorrow, fear and hope, longing, awe, mystery, hesitation, with which classicism had remained content, it strives constantly to define more narrowly, to particularize, to isolate, and hence moves constantly away from the epical in style toward the lyrical. The brief lyric is the form which all the composers of this school favor, and in which they best succeed: we find it in Schubert's songs, in Schumann's novelettes and Chopin's nocturnes, in Mendelssohn's songs without words, in Grieg's lyric pieces, and in our own day in the preludes and other pieces of Debussy. These all aim at vivid characterization of a single feeling or mood; they are flash-light pictures, landscapes seen by lightning; they show little effort after development, contrast, or composition. They are in music what the *genre* picture is in painting, the short story in literature.

We have seen many signs of the same individualist tendency in Beethoven. Not only did we observe his sturdy personal independence in all matters of ordinary life—in costume, in manners, in political and religious opinion—but we noted how in his music he often sacrificed the serene classic beauty in order to express himself with more intensity, how in such a work as the "Pathétique Sonata," he entered what we call the "romantic world of personal feeling."* Every one of his nine symphonies is vividly characterized; the third is heroic, the fifth tragic, the sixth rustic, the seventh humorous (with the humor of giants), the ninth religious, and so on. We even note in him the beginning of the romantic fondness for titles: The "Pathetic Sonata," the "Heroic Symphony," the piano sonata of "Departure, Absence, and Return." Later composers, especially the literary Schumann, carried this much further, as we shall see, not resting content with such bizarre titles as "The Bird as Prophet," and "Why?", but introducing mottoes and quotations in his pieces, and even signing them with initials standing for various aspects of his temperament. In orchestral music this tendency to the individual and the picturesque was less

*"The Appreciation of Music," page 168.

Chap. I

evident, but shows itself in an interesting and unexpected way in the overtures of the "landscape painter" Mendelssohn, as Wagner called him—the "Midsummer Night's Dream" and the "Hebrides."

IV

Folk-music and nationalism.

In the same composer's two best-known symphonies, the "Scottish" and the "Italian," we observe another phase of romanticism—its keen interest in local color, in national peculiarities as they are reflected in folk-song. Beethoven had used a Russian theme in one of his quartets, even Haydn had used many of the folk-songs of the Croatians in his symphonies, but it remained for Chopin, in his mazurkas, polonaises, and other Polish dances, for Liszt in his Hungarian rhapsodies, for Grieg in his Norwegian dances, and for Dvořák* in his works founded on Bohemian tunes, to celebrate the geographical individual, so to speak, as other romanticists celebrated the personal one. Musical literature has thus been greatly the gainer, for remote and little-known types of melody exert the same charm that fascinates us in picturesque costumes and outlandish manners. Many modern composers not studied in these articles owe much of their interest to their use of folk-song. The Bohemian Smetana was in this respect the forerunner of Dvořák. Albeniz and others have drawn on the rich stores of native Spanish music. Tschaïkowsky slightly, but much

*A Bohemian name, pronounced Dvorzhahk.

more Rimsky-Korsakoff, Borodine, and Moussorgsky, have given us the melancholy songs of Russian peasants. In our own country MacDowell, Chadwick, Mr. Henry F. Gilbert and others, as well as Dvořák during his residence here, have based some of their compositions on negro and Indian tunes.

V

Romantic types of structure.

The interest the romanticist takes in the vivid presentment of the single mood or aspect naturally leads him to subordinate or neglect everything else; he brings his object into sharp focus and leaves all else vague; he necessarily ignores its relationships and possible developments. This is said not in adverse criticism of his type of art, but in order to distinguish it clearly from the other more classic type in which contrast, balance, and development play so much more prominent a part. Just as we compared the lyric piece of the romanticist to the modern short story, we may compare the sonata or symphony to the novel; and the analogy is so close that the literary comparison may help the reader to understand the musical one. The short-story writer—Kipling, Stevenson, or de Maupassant, for example, works by isolating one character, scene, or incident from all its relations, and presenting it to us as it exists, statically and without change, at a given moment, as vividly as he can. The novelist, on the contrary, as George Eliot in "Middlemarch," or George Meredith in "The Egoist," regards his char-

CHAP. I

The symphony and the novel.

acters not statically, but dynamically, as constantly changing and growing, and this chiefly through their action and reaction on one another. Instead of isolating, he combines. Now, this is precisely the difference between the composer of a character piece and the composer of a sonata. The first aims altogether at singleness of impression, at the presentation of a static, self-complete musical idea. The second tries rather to put three or four contrasting characters (themes) on his musical stage, and to let them gradually work out their own drama before us, both by self-development and by reciprocal action.

As all structure in art is determined by the nature of the ideas to be embodied, it is clear that the constructive types needed for the static, self-complete themes of the romanticist will be quite different from that best fitted to evolving, interactive musical ideas—namely, the sonata. This theoretical conclusion is verified by history. Not only do we find the typical romanticists confining themselves chiefly to brief pieces, but when they write longer ones, or sonatas or symphonies, they are apt to be successful only in proportion as they break wholly with tradition. Schumann is an instructive study in this respect. In his early piano pieces he hits upon exactly the concise self-complete forms needed for his ideas: each is a minute cell, a self-closed circuit; and even when the composition seems of some length, as in the novelettes or the "Carnaval" or the

Music in "water-tight compartments."

"Kreisleriana," it resolves itself on examination into a series or mosaic of these cells, a vessel, so to speak, made up of many watertight compartments. But when he tried to apply the same method to his symphonies, where the larger orchestral canvas absolutely demanded a freer sweep of brush, it was quite inadequate, and we find him helplessly repeating bits of his melodies, charming in themselves, but quickly becoming wearisome in this reiteration. Schubert also repeats much, in his symphonies, where Beethoven would have developed. It is a commonplace of criticism that Chopin's sonatas, beautiful as the music in them is, are not, properly speaking, sonatas at all. Neither are Grieg's. Berlioz, for all his wonderful orchestral color, wrote very unsymphonic symphonies, and it is indeed not until we reach Franck, Brahms, and Strauss that we find symphonic music taking on again the sustained, evolving, dynamic character it had in classic times.

VI

The interest in color.

By a natural compensation, the romantic composers excel their classic fathers in richness, variety, and subtlety of sensuous color as much as they fall short of them in the power of sustained thought. Preoccupation with thought is not always favorable to persuasive charm in its presentation, and a felicitous use of the peculiar properties of each artistic medium comes only with a specialization in technique not likely to be undertaken by men more intent on what they say than on how they say it. Thus Bach, for example, writes often for instruments as if they were voices, and for instruments of quite dissimilar mechanism as if they were alike, as when he gives the same melody to violins and oboes at the same time. Such "doubling" of one line in the texture by instruments of different sound production and tone quality, whenever it results in an uncertainty of color comparable to the muddiness of mixed pigments in painting, is repugnant to the modern ear. To what different methods leads the principle of pure color for each line may be seen by ten minutes' study of any orchestral score of such master colorists as Wagner, Tschaïkowsky, Dvořák, or Strauss. In piano music the same change of attitude is noticeable. Beethoven, however carefully he planned the march of his harmonies, placed them often so low in register that they growl and grate most unpleasantly. Schumann, Mendelssohn, and, above all, Chopin, developed the capacity of the left hand and availed themselves of the aid of the pedal in such a way as to improve surprisingly the sound of such passages, as we shall see later in more detail. Almost the entire value of a composer like Debussy, comparable to the impressionists of the sister art of painting, depends on his peculiar and elusive effects of color.

VII

Programme music.

All this modern development of color, however, may have, of course, little or no necessary connection with romanticism. It may well be argued that its relation to romanticism is one of accidental contemporaneity rather than of effect and cause; that had classicism held undisputed sway it would still have occurred; and that it was only the natural result of the mechanical perfecting of instruments and the growing specialization of the style appropriate to each, without any reference whatever to musical æsthetics. Its relation to the romantic movement is in any case much more casual and less intimate than that of the tendency to special expression. That is intrinsic; wherever we find romanticism in music we find this tendency to specialize the expression. And so, when we get the extreme of such specialization of expression, the ultimate literal precision beyond which music cannot go, we have romanticism in its most radical form, giving rise to what is called "programme music." Here it reaches a critical point, at which it transcends itself and passes over into realism.

The "Coriolanus" overture.

In order fully to appreciate how much greater is the distance traversed by music in passing from romanticism to realism than that which separates romanticism from its classic origin we must retrace our steps a moment. As we have already seen, the difference between classic and romantic is more one of emphasis than of kind. The writer has pointed out elsewhere* that such a composition as Beethoven's "Coriolanus" Overture may be considered either classic or romantic, according to the standpoint from which we regard it. If we listen to it as the expression of two contrasting emotions, one of restlessness and agitation, the other of pleading gentleness, it is classic.† If we recall the title and the story of Coriolanus, the exiled Roman general, who was dissuaded from an attack on Rome by the prayers of his wife and mother, then the first theme will symbolize for us Coriolanus's hate, and the second the women's pleading, and the overture as a whole will be romantic, because specifically expressive. In other words, both classic and romantic music deal with subjective emotions, the difference being that in the former their interpretation is left to the hearer's imagination, in the latter it is indicated by a title or "label."

Again, the structural types used for romantic music are essentially of the same kind as those of the classic period. The sonata form used in Mendelssohn's "Hebrides" and Schumann's "Manfred" overtures is the same that had already served Haydn, Mozart, and Beethoven. It is true that the smaller types are

*"A Guide to Music," Chapter VIII, "Music That Tells Stories," pp. 91-93.

†The reader must be on his guard against the popular fallacy that classical music is "unemotional." The mere fact that its emotions are not labelled does not detract from their power. Indeed, it may enhance it, by leaving our imaginations free to interpret as they will.

often more suitable to what the romanticist has to say than the more elaborate ones, but, nevertheless, the methods of organization are essentially the same in all.

Programme music is narrative.

Now, programme music differs much more radically from classic music than this, both in content and in modes of construction. Its content is no longer a single poetic idea, but a story, a series of events to be followed out literally and in detail. It is thus narrative rather than lyric. For example, Beethoven, who anticipated programme music as well as so many other modern developments, gives us in his "Pastoral Symphony" not merely the poetic idea, the feeling, of the country (though that is indeed the subject of the first movement), but an account of a whole series of rustic happenings: the meditation by the brook, the songs of the birds, the merry-making of the peasants, the thunder-storm, the shepherd's song of joy. Berlioz is even more detailed, Strauss still more so. If the romantic composer gives us a label, the realist provides us with complete "Directions for Using." Such a definite series of events as he deals in, strictly following a necessary order, and illuminated by more or less objective imitation by the music of the objects described, is as different as possible from the subjective emotions which form the subject matter alike of the romanticist and of the classicist.

Structurally the programmists departed as widely from tradition. Berlioz saw clearly that structural types like the sonata could not be reconciled to the constant change involved in musical narrative, but he was unable to devise a scheme both sufficiently elastic and definite enough to be clear. Wagner complained of the wandering effect of his music. Liszt, as we shall see, did much pioneer work toward elaborating the type we know as the "symphonic poem," the principle of which is to follow freely the phases of the "story," or programme, but at the same time to maintain musical unity and clearness by constant reference to the fundamental themes in divers transformations. Strauss and others have built on the foundations thus laid by Liszt.

VII

These distinctions will later become clearer.

The many rather subtle and difficult distinctions that have been made in this chapter may perhaps puzzle students unaccustomed to æsthetic theory, and especially those unfamiliar with the actual examples of musical composition from the study of which these theoretical discriminations have been drawn. Such students may rest assured that all these distinctions will become much clearer to them as they read the following chapters. After finishing the book they may then return to a reconsideration of the attempt at classification which has here been made. Meanwhile, the following table may serve them as a rough indication of the main divisions of our subject:

CLASSIFICATION OF MUSICAL TYPES

MUSIC

VOCAL

Specifies content by text.

INSTRUMENTAL

ABSOLUTE OR CLASSIC

Deals with subjective emotions, unlabelled.
Structural types traditional.
Example: Beethoven's "Fifth Symphony."

ROMANTIC AND REALISTIC

ROMANTIC

Deals with single "poetic" subject, indicated by title, conveyed through subjective emotion.
Structural types traditional.
Examples: Schumann's "Why?" Mendelssohn's "Hebrides" Overture.

REALISTIC

("Programme Music")

Deals with a complete series of events, enumerated in the programme.
Examples: Berlioz's "Symphonie Fantastique." Strauss's "Till Eulenspiegel."

CHAPTER II

Franz Schubert

RANZ PETER SCHUBERT, often called the first of the romanticists, although, as we have seen, his predecessors were also romanticists whenever they expressed personal rather than general emotion in their music, was born in Vienna, January 31, 1797, and died in the same city, where he had passed practically the whole of his short life, November 19, 1828. He was descended from a family of Moravian peasants. His father was a schoolmaster, and his mother was in domestic service before her marriage. Franz was the thirteenth child of this union. As several of the children were musically gifted, it was early the family custom to play together Sunday afternoons to an audience of relatives and neighbors. While Schubert was a student at the Imperial School it was his habit to return home every week for these quartet parties, where he played the viola, his father the violoncello, and two of his brothers the violins. By degrees other instruments were added, and the quartet grew into

Schubert's environment.

a small orchestra. Later the players organized into the Orchestral Society of Amateurs, larger quarters were obtained, and symphony programmes were given. It was for this society that Schubert wrote his fourth and fifth symphonies.

A spontaneous musician.

Born into an industrious, simple, music-loving family, Schubert seems to have grown from childhood to boyhood and youth, exercising his musical genius as spontaneously as a flower turns to the light. The story of his musical development is the story of his life. He began to play as soon as he was tall enough to reach the piano keys, and he began to write tunes as soon as he could write the notes. No record was kept of his earliest compositions, but a piano sonata for four hands (D major), written when he was eight years old, is often played, and his piano fantasia for four hands (there were plenty of hands available in the family) was written in his thirteenth year. His disposition and temperament, as well as his extraordinary genius, were not unlike Mozart's; but his life was much less eventful and his surroundings simpler. Consequently, childlike as was Mozart, Schubert was even more so. He knew nothing of the ways of the world, and had no worldly ambition. As a man he was unaffected, affectionate, honest and sincere. He was merely the source of his music, which gushed forth as spontaneously as water from a fountain. It is only in the music of the last years of his short life that we can see his intellectual reaction on his environ-

Chap. II

ment; and it was but a few days before his death that, realizing his need of training in counterpoint, he went to Sechter, the famous teacher, and arranged for lessons. What would have been the result of such training, and of the introspective awakening which his realization of his need of it implies, we can only imagine. But that his contemporaries expected much from his future can be seen by the inscription on his grave, which reads: "Music has here entombed a rich treasure, but still more glorious hopes."

II

His songs.

It is not surprising that, as music was to Schubert an instinctive reaction upon feeling, he should find perfect expression in the song. The song is the vivid presentment of a single emotion or mood. No sustained intellectual power or development of ideas is needed. It is the short story in music, and, like the short story of literature, it aims to express the dramatic apex of an emotion or mood. All else sinks into vague insignificance. No elaborate interaction of causes and effects, of ideas and feelings, is needed or desired; the essence of an emotion or of a particular mood is depicted or expressed, and that is enough. Schubert's temperament and genius were particularly suited for such lyric expression. He was as sensitive, as intense in his feelings, as a child, and music was his instinctive speech. As he felt, his thought was clothed in music. It is said that a lady once handed him a poem to read, suggesting that he make a song of it. He went to a window and stood rereading it a few times, then exclaimed: "I have it; it is already composed!" His exquisite song, "Hark! Hark! the Lark," with its beautiful accompaniment, flashed into his mind in a like instantaneous way, when he happened to pick up a volume of "Cymbeline" at a restaurant table, and the sketch of the music was written on the back of a bill of fare. The same evening, at the restaurant, he read, and what we can only call discovered, or felt, the music for the verses of "Who Is Sylvia?", that tender questioning of the lover's heart.

"The most poetic of musicians."

The vividness, power and variety of Schubert's pictures of emotions and moods are marvellous. Liszt called him "le musicien le plus poetique," and Schumann said, in explaining how inevitable were his musical reactions, "He could have set a wall-advertisement to music." His genius responded automatically to the particular emotions called upon. Not all of his songs are lyric expressions, like "Hark! Hark! the Lark," "Sylvia," the "Serenade" and "Am Meer," in which the music is the embodiment of the general mood; occasionally he reinforced the dramatic action of the words of the poem by imitations in the music, as in the "Erl-King," "The Wanderer," "Die Allmacht" and others. Some of these latter are great songs of their kind, but in others, where the poem set was theatric rather than truly dramatic, or where Schubert has perhaps exceeded the bounds of his literary imagination, he was less successful, tending to overuse conventional devices, like the tremolo accompaniment, and harmonies based on the diminished seventh chord. In any song which Schubert felt sincerely, his musical expression follows the emotion with a marvellous elasticity. In gay passages he finds himself in the major mode; in an expression of sadness he falls into the minor. His modulations are not made by rule, but are an impulse of genius. His music lapses from key to key, as spontaneously as the expression of the human face follows the thought of the mind.

Expressiveness of his accompaniments.

It was not only in the melody for the singer that the poet's feeling was mirrored, but the accompaniment was used as an expressive instrument. He thought intuitively of the poem, the melody and the accompaniment as the combined interpretation of an emotion, and used them together with perfect freedom. In "The Trout" we have a representation of the jumping fish as a basis of the piano part, while throughout "The Organ-grinder" we hear in the bass the wheezy drone of the barrel-organ. Since each new emotion or mood demanded or implied its own expression, he discarded in his more elaborate songs the "strophic" method, where several stanzas are given with the same melody and accompaniment, and used what the Germans call the "through-composed" method, where the changing feelings of the different stanzas are embodied in different melodies and accompaniments, bound into unity by the same laws which make the unity of the poem, or by some natural musical logic, such as the repetition of the principal motive at the close of the song. The original artistry of this is evident when we consider the naïveté of the repetitions in the folk-songs on which Schubert's method were largely based. In Silcher's "Die Lorelei," for example, the same air is placidly repeated over and over, no matter how tragic the text may become. "The Wanderer" and "Lindenbaum" are two particularly happy examples of Schubert's instinct in this matter.

Lapses in declamation.

In qualification, it may be noted as peculiarly characteristic of Schubert's easy-going ways, that once his musical imagination was released by the words, he sometimes paid scant attention to them, letting the stream of musical thought carry him on, regardless of the lines. His "declamation" is often faulty. An amusing instance of this can be found in "Death and the Maiden," where, in addressing the figure of Death, the maiden cries, instead of "Go! wild and skinless man," "Go wild! and skinless man," which sounds more sensible than it is. In "Wandering," again, he adopts at the outset a musical phrase necessitating a repetition of the final syllables in the line. This works very well in the first stanza, where the idea thus emphasized is "to wander"; but the device is less happy when we have to repeat "the millstone" and other prosaic names.

"Hark! Hark! the Lark," jotted down by Schubert, as we have seen, in a café, on the

Chap. II

Examples for analysis, Nos. 1, 2 and 3

Hark! Hark! the Lark!" "Der Doppelgänger." "Am Meer."

back of a bill of fare, in the excitement aroused by Shakespeare's beautiful lyric from "Cymbeline," is certainly one of the finest songs in all music. The spontaneity and grace of the melody are remarkable even for Schubert; rhythm, harmony and modulation all contribute to the general effect; and in every detail there is a perfection of workmanship, a felicity, precision and restraint which he seldom attained. Some composers have believed that the melody of a song should be able to stand by itself, intelligible without its accompaniment. That is a severe and sometimes an unfair test, but "Hark! Hark! the Lark" comes out of it victorious. How many beauties there are in the melodic line, quite apart from harmony and the rhythms of the accompaniment! How perfect is the equilibrium of the tune as a whole, the sense it gives of unity in all its variety! And how many charming details one encounters from line to line, almost from word to word!

The first phrase, for example, measures 9 and 10,* is repeated in the third, measures 13-14,—but not literally;—as if in the elation of its beauty it took a new curve. The second phrase is also echoed in the fourth, but with a wider lift on the final syllable, completed by the lovely curve of the cadence in measure 17. Then, with one of those sudden modulations Schubert loves for their magic

*Number the measures from the start of the piano prelude, ignoring, however, the single beat at the beginning.

of color, there is a phrase or two in G flat major, after which the original key of B flat is as easily, almost casually, reëntered, and, with a slight repetition, the climax reaches its acme on the word "Arise," three times repeated, with a slight compensating diminution of force supplied by the downward direction of the high notes. After this in turn has been repeated, the whole is ended by another most graceful cadence (measures 37-38).

"Der Doppelgänger" belongs to a completely different type of song from "Hark! Hark! the Lark," and makes its effect hardly at all by melody, almost entirely by harmony, tone-color and text. It is not lyric, but dramatic. It tells the story of a lover who fancies he sees his own double standing in the moonlight outside the house where his sweetheart used to live. The voice part is not melodic, but freely declamatory. The steady musical pulse is supplied, not by it, but by the sombre chords in the low register of the piano, succeeding each other with the relentlessness of fate and rising to harsh clangor or sinking to mournful undertone in obedience to an art that must be studied to be duly admired. The last eight measures, after the voice has stopped entirely, are particularly fine. The four-measure phrase, whose recurrence is the structural principle of unity in the song, takes on in this final case a new severity from the lowering of its last note (C sharp to C). The ending in B major instead of minor is again exceedingly original. "Der Doppelgänger" is de-

CHAP. II

servedly one of its composer's most celebrated songs of dramatic character.

"Am Meer," written but three months before Schubert's premature death, presents an interesting combination of the lyric and the dramatic method. Its melody, like that of "Hark! Hark!" and unlike that of "Der Doppelgänger," will stand alone, and, indeed, contains some very beautiful phrases from a purely musical standpoint. Yet it is equally clear that the composer is primarily concerned here, not with musical beauty, but with truth, even minute truth, to his text. Thus only are to be explained the tremolo in the accompaniment that ushers in the second and fourth stanzas, with their tragic content, the plangent dissonances that accompany their cadences. Less programmistic, but far more poetically suggestive, are the chords which begin and end the song. "They speak," says Mr. Philip Hale, "of the sea at nightfall."

The student should analyze as many examples as possible, especially of the better known songs, such as the "Serenade," "Who Is Sylvia?" "The Wanderer," "The Erl King," "Du Bist die Ruh," "Mignon's Song," "Death and the Maiden," "Gretchen am Spinnrade," "The Young Nun."

III

Piano and instrumental works.

The same qualities which make Schubert preëminent as a song-writer show in his piano music, and also, more distinctly, the love of color characteristic of the romanticist. In his instinctive appreciation of the value of kaleidoscopic harmonies, dissolving dissonances and unexpected modulations, Schubert was the precursor of Schumann, Chopin and Debussy. But of his piano works, as of his orchestral works, the opinion would be less unanimous than of his songs. If we look at Schubert with the eye of the romanticist, we have nothing but wonder and admiration for his truly marvelous lyrical gift, exemplified hardly more in his songs than in his quartets and symphonies. If we look at him from another standpoint, that of a man to whom constructive power in art is as indispensable as what is vaguely called "inspiration," we find it necessary heavily to qualify our praise. No one can dare to say what were the bounds of Schubert's natural genius in music, but his limitations as an artist are easily evident. His melodies and themes were poured forth from what seemed an inexhaustible source, but they remained as they originally came forth. He did not labor to make his melodies grow, as most of the great artists have done. He used them with comparatively little variation, as he first found them, repeating them again and again in their original form. His natural endowment was so great as actually to hinder his artistic growth. He lacked the necessity for intellectual struggle. A friend once showed him Beethoven's note-books, where page after page of tentative working-out of the themes showed the master's patient labor to attain the perfect blossoming of his idea, and his comment was, "If

His facility a disadvantage.

composing is such hard work as that, I don't want to compose."

Add to the disadvantage of his wonderful facility the fact that his contented nature did not drive him into the spiritual revolt against his sordid circumstances which might have roused his energies, and one can understand his apparent inertia. He was satisfied to write the music that poured into his mind with no effort but to let the notes flow from his pen. It was only shortly before his death that he began to realize the possibility of yet undiscovered depths in his own genius, possibilities which he must work to reveal. In his later music there is an intensity of utterance—a nervous energy which contrasts strongly with the genial prolixity of the earlier. He is beginning to disencumber his individuality, to express the reaction of his genius on the tragedy of existence. There is a tenseness here which is distinctly modern; the D-minor Quartet, particularly, has the modern closeness of texture and rapidity of pulse. Indeed, as an artist, Schubert never reaches greater heights than in his chamber music, where, with the few instruments at his command, he discloses a new world of dramatic expression and emotional depth.

The symphonist.

As a symphonist, Schubert showed the same qualities which made him preëminent as a song-writer. The freshness, lyrical expressiveness and warm beauty of his themes make us hear in them constantly that quality of the human voice which Schumann heard. His scores are wonderfully rich in color and impressionistic in their orchestral tints. No one knows better than he how to make the oboe sultry and menacing, the clarinet mellow and liquid, the horn hollow, vague, mystical, the 'cellos passionate, and the violins clear, aspiring and ethereal. And, finally, the very profusion of his thought gives his work in the larger forms its own kind of heroism of style. It is not closely woven, nervous work, like Beethoven's; it is not highly organized and intellectual, like Brahms's; it has not even the passionate intensity of Schumann's; but it has an amplitude, a wide sweep, a wealth of beauty, that make it truly heroic, and that Schumann had in mind when he characterized the C-major Symphony as of "heavenly length." His limitations are equally personal. His themes are more often lyrical than deeply significant, more personal than universal. His music does not evolve and grow from its own innate vitality. It is rather like a chain of perfect crystals than like the temple of beauty which a more constructive genius might have built for us. But his last symphony, the great C-major, shows a reserve of power not associated with Schubert the song-writer. Here is a scope of intention, a sustained imagination, that rank it with the splendid art works of all time.

Example for analysis, No. 4. The Unfinished Symphony, the first movement.

When Schubert was twenty-five years old he wrote for a musical society at Gratz the *Allegro moderato* and the *Andante con moto* which we know by the name of the Unfinished Symphony, together with a few bars of a scherzo. It is a remarkable work, undoubtedly one of the finest symphonies since Beethoven. It breathes a romantic warmth of sentiment peculiar to Schubert; it is like a long and varied song or serenade; nor is it devoid, especially in the development section and the coda, of the nobility and seriousness suitable to symphonic style.

The first theme begins with a melody of somber expression, for the low basses, without harmony, which contains in its two characteristic motives the germs of the important developments to come. (Motive *a,* as we may call it, measures 1 to 3. Motive *b,* measures 3 to 5.) For the moment this subject is stated and dismissed, and the music goes on with a curious undulating figure in the violins over a bass in persistent rhythm, against which presently silhouettes itself, so to speak, a graceful Schubertian melody in clarinet and oboe. The scheme of color here is charming, each of the three well-contrasted elements—sustained tune of the wind instruments, undulation of violins and iterant figure of basses—contributing its quota to an unforgettable ensemble. There is a slight climax and a long, curiosity-piqueing hold on D (measures 38, 39, 40). What is going to happen? What happens is that the two horns and two bassoons which attacked this D as the third step in the scale of B minor, diverge from it as the dominant of the key of G, with an effect the charm of which is indescribable. It is one of the composer's most felicitous intuitions of color. The well-known 'cello melody which constitutes the second theme follows, first in the 'cellos (measures 44-52), and later in the violins (53-61). This time the expected cadence is dramatically interrupted by a full-measure pause and an onslaught of turbulent chords. This in turn gives place to attractive "imitations" of a figure from the second theme (measure 46) in measures 73 to 84, and to still more delightful imitations of the opening phrase of the theme in measures 94 to 103.

The development begins with a reiteration of the main theme, now in the subdominant key of E minor (measures 115-122). Then, taking the first motive of this, Schubert subjects it to a varied and interesting treatment. First he "imitates" it from one instrument to another. Then he inverts it, so that it moves downward instead of upward (measures 135 *et seq.*), the rapidity of the movement meanwhile increasing and leading to interesting displacements of accent. The outcome of all this agitation is an impressively massive restatement of the theme, measures 171-176. Motive *a* recommences in the bass in the two following measures, with a new whirling figure in the violins, strangely exciting, as a foil. With measure 185 comes another phase, motive *b* imitated from bass (185-187) to treble (187-189) against a "dotted" rhythm (dotted eighths and sixteenths) that still further fans the excitement. A final crisis ends in subsidence, and with measure 219 begins the reëxposition of the themes. It will be noted that the development thus hastily examined is not only remarkably skilful technically for a composer of twenty-five, but is emotionally fresh in a way that no "made-to-order" development can ever be. The themes really act, they are not merely badgered and worried. Hence the fine effect of the section as a whole.

Not so much can be said for the recapitulation of themes. It is the weakest point in the movement. The clarinet and oboe solo above undulating violins is particularly drawn out—wearisomely so. It seems almost as if Schubert did not know how to reach the A which is to usher in his second theme. At least, he goes for it by a roundabout route—and that at the very moment where a short cut is most desirable, and would certainly have been taken by Beethoven. The second theme, too, for all its beauty, seems a bit diffuse the second time, almost literally repeated, note for note, even to the measure of silence. A short but impressive coda brings to an end what must be considered, despite all qualifications, one of the finest example of symphonic music that we owe to the romantic composers.

CHAPTER III

Robert Schumann

Attitude toward music.

IN Robert Schumann (1810-1856) we find the greatest genius and the most fascinating personality of the Romantic School. More intellectual and subjective than Schubert, more keenly emotional than Mendelssohn, more virile and balanced than Chopin, he stands at the apex of the group, consciously expressing himself and his time in the medium of music. Whereas Schubert's feeling was instinctively, almost unconsciously, reflected in his works, Schumann found in his art an elastic medium for his thought, and adapted it as carefully to the subtleties of his reflections as the literary artist molds his phrases and his sentences to his ideas. His music was the reflection not only of his feeling, but of his reasoned reflection on his feeling. It was the expression equally of his heart and of his intellect. Coming in this way from the depths of his individuality, it was never imitative. He never went through the period of playing the "sedulous ape," as do most artists. For him form was of little importance compared with content, and the study of the laws of music was only a means to give genius a mastery of its tools. Not that he undervalued the great masters or underestimated the advantage of the study of their works. Never was there a more loving, even reverent, admirer of Bach, or a more ardent student of his music. But he felt that Bach was great primarily because he had great things to express, and that his methods were but the means to the end. It was perhaps because of this emphasis on music as an expression that he found a peculiar sympathy with Bach rather than with Mozart or Beethoven, who wrote at a time when the formal side of music had reached a more perfected development.

Literary tendencies.

His use of music as an expression of particular and personal emotion was developed in him in connection with a marked literary taste, an ability inherited perhaps from his father, a book publisher and the translator of Byron's and Scott's works into German. The two arts of poetry and music seemed inextricably mingled in his thought. His attempt seemed always to be to make music express what language means, exactly the reverse of Hoffmann's attempt a few years earlier to make words express music, but showing the same sense of the interchangeability of the arts. Indeed, as a child, his precocity was fully as marked in his literary interest as in his music. He early fell under the influence of Jean Paul Richter, to whom he later acknowledged his artistic debt, saying, "I learned more counterpoint from Jean Paul than from my music master." In fact, he was directly influenced by Richter's ideas in many of his compositions, notably "Kreisleriana" and the "Papillons," apropos of which he writes his friend Henrietta Voigt: "I might tell you a good deal about them had not Jean Paul done it so much better. If you ever have a moment to spare please read the last chapter of the 'Flegeljähre,' where you will find it all in black and white, down to the seven league boot, in F-sharp minor."—and so on, in some detail.

Up to his sixteenth year all his budding artistic gifts were fostered by his father's interest and assistance, but after August Schumann's death in 1826 his situation was materially altered. Frau Schumann, a capable, practical woman, unhesitatingly declared against any artistic career and insisted that her son take up the study of law. It was only after some years spent ostensibly at legal studies, although in reality his best energies were even then reserved for piano practice and the study of composition, that he was able to persuade his mother and his guardian to allow him definitely to adopt music as his profession. He immediately began piano lessons under Friedrich Wieck in Leipsic, intending to study to become a piano virtuoso. Unfortunately for his ambition, but fortunately for the world, which gained a great composer when it lost a pianist, he attempted to find a short cut to technical dexterity by using a mechanical invention of his own to increase the independence of the fourth finger. The result was fatal. He practically lost the use of his finger, and was obliged to renounce the career of a pianist forever. He does not seem to have been much afflicted by this incident, for in the same letter in which he informs one of his friends of it he adds, "My prospects are very bright. My reception in the world of art could not have been more encouraging."

II

Youthful enthusiasm.

He immediately began the composition of many piano pieces, all more or less exemplifying his belief that music should give free rein to the fancy, and that imaginative expression must not be sacrificed even for beauty of design. To his early twenties belong the Abegg Variations, the "Papillons," the "Davidsbündlertänze," the "Toccata," the "Carnaval," the "Etudes Symphoniques," the F-sharp minor Sonata, all bubbling with fresh melody, vigorous rhythms, and daring harmonies, and most of them intended not only as beautiful music, but as the specific expression of the composer's moods or ideas. Frequently they were accompanied by a sort of programme, explanatory notes, or suggestive comments, as, for instance, in the first edition of the "Davidsbündlertänze," where the music is interlarded with such phrases as, "Here Florestan stops, his lips trembling painfully," and "Eusebius said too much about this; but his eyes were full of joy." Indeed, most of his youthful music is filled with ingenious and amusing allusions to places and people for the edification of the initiated. Sometimes, as in the Abegg Variations, the theme is founded on letters, in this case on the pseudonym of a friend of Schumann's; sometimes the allusion is given in a fanciful title or poetic motto; most elaborate of all is the fanciful play in the "Davidsbündlertänze," music written for the imaginary club which figured so largely in Schumann's literary contributions to the "Neue Zeitschrift," and which was composed entirely of fictitious characters representing his friends or exemplifying different sides of his own character. For instance, "Florestan" was the gay and lively Schumann, "Eusebius" the thoughtful Schumann, while Clara Wieck was disguised as "Chiarina," and Mendelssohn, the last man in the world to be found in such fantastic company had he been given his choice, appeared as "Felix Meritis."

And freshness of invention.

But what has kept this music alive is not this elaborate paraphernalia or the fairy-tales with which it was associated in Schumann's mind, but the entrancing charm of the music itself. The inexhaustible freshness of melody is little short of marvelous. For the most part, the motives are brief and striking phrases presented one after the other with all the kaleidoscopic beauty which subtleties of rhythm and endless varieties of harmonic devices can give them. Many of the audacities of Schumann's harmonies were due to his sensuous susceptibility to good ear-filling sound. Sir Hubert Parry says, "He loved to use all the pedal that was possible, and had little objection to hearing all the notes of the scale sounding at once. He is said to have liked dreaming to himself, by rambling through all sorts of harmonies with the pedal down, and the glamour of crossing rhythms and the sound of clashing and antagonistic notes was most thoroughly adapted to his nature."

In his early pieces are preserved many curious experiments in such clashing sonorities, some very successful and others less so, but all highly original. Two examples may be mentioned. "Paganini" of the "Carnaval" ends with four crashing double thirds, so low in register that they make less a musical sound than an ear-splitting discord. While this is still resounding, the soft, dominant seventh chord of A flat (see Figure I, a) is taken, and the moment the pedal is changed "comes out" through the jangle like a lantern through a fog. "Papillons" ends with an even more ingenious effect (Figure I, b). The dominant seventh chord of D is rolled by both hands and held; then, beginning at the bottom, one note after another is released, until only the top one remains. The result is that the ear becomes conscious of each note *by its cessation,* instead of by its beginning, as is ordinarily the case. One seems to be hearing the ghost of a chord disappearing into space.

Figure I.

Taken all together, these early piano compositions reveal an extraordinarily mobile and fanciful temperament, working with the greatest freedom and spontaneity, though without the guidance of rigorous discipline. There are undeniable crudities and the style is highly subjective, eccentric, and arbitrary. Yet there is such unflagging vitality, such rare and various beauty, that one would not sacrifice them for works many times more technically perfect.

Example for analysis, No. 5. Selected pieces from the "Carnaval," Opus 9. (Composed 1834 and 1835.)

This set of twenty-one pieces, of which we shall examine only a few of the most characteristic, represents the youthful Schumann in his happiest vein. As its title suggests, it is a sort of review of the motley fancies and impressions that troop through his brain. Its musical continuity is of the slightest, so that even when it is interpreted by the most sympathetic artists it does not uninterruptedly hold the attention, and it leaves rather a confused impression behind it. On the other hand, it is packed full of beauties, of charming effects, of happy "finds," with which even Schumann—even the young Schumann—is not often so lavish.

Of course, it is provided with a fairly elaborate literary machinery. Not only do the titles refer to a hundred ideas outside of the music, such as the composer's friends (Chopin, Estrella—in real life Ernestine von Fricken, and Chiarina—in real life Clara Wieck), aspects of his own personality (Eusebius, Florestan), and the legendary characters of carnival, such as Pierrot, Harlequin, Pantaloon, and Columbine, but there is a musical motto which plays an important rôle, the theme of four notes mentioned in the sub-title—"Scenes mignonnes sur quatre notes." This consists of the notes A, E flat, C, and B, the German names of which, A, S, C, H, spell the name of a town in which lived one of Schumann's friends. He was fond of this playful spelling with the musical letters, and has used A-B-E-G-G in his Variations, opus 1, B-A-C-H in some fugues on that great name, A-D-E, G-A-D-E ("Gade, Farewell") in a piece dedicated to the Danish composer on his departure from Germany, and other words in the same way.

The brilliant introduction ("Préambule") is notable for its Schumannesque vigor of rhythm, and for its quick and complete changes of mood (note the charm of the wistful, almost coy "animato" in contrast with the headlong dash of the section marked "più moto").

FIGURE II.

In "Pierrot" we first meet the four notes of the motto, A, E flat, C, B—in this case the B is represented by C flat—first in the left hand, then in the right (Figure II, a), in a simple rhythm of even notes. This piece is punctuated, so to speak, throughout by a little descending phrase of three notes, first heard in the third measure. There is endless charm in the way these notes constantly recur, with varying harmonies.

"Harlequin," true to his traditional character, transforms the motto into a more florid form. (Figure II, b.) It may be noted that the composer uses his motto only to get his theme in each piece, to jog his imagination; once he has the theme he develops it with complete independence and with much fertility of fancy.

"Eusebius" is a picture of the thoughtful side of Schumann—a lovely quiet piece, markedly subjective, and containing only a rather veiled reference to the motto.

In contrast with its tranquil beauty, Florestan—the impulsive Schumann—is full of unquenchable high spirits. The motto here forms a new melody. (Figure II, c.) A curious feature is the quotation, at the ninth measure, of a part of the composer's own earlier work, "Papillons," opus 2.

If "Coquette" had been left without title, we could almost guess its name from the seductive rhythmic outline that the motto now takes. (Figure II, d.)

And if it is coquettish here it seems to take wings and fly away in number 9, "Papillons" ("Butterflies")—Figure II, e.

Indeed, we can compare it to a butterfly also in the many transformations it passes through without losing its identity—transformations too many for us to follow here in detail. Only glancing, then, at the whimsical grace of "Lettres dansantes," at the languid loveliness of "Chopin," at the light charm of "Reconnaissance" with its reiterated thumb-notes, we may pass directly to the finale, the March of the David Club against the Philistines. The heavy, unenlightened philistine spirit is here symbolized by an old tune of the seventeenth century, the "Grandfather's Dance," first heard in the bass in the fifty-fourth measure. Passages from the Préambule are reintroduced for the sake of unity, and of course the David Club, representing sweetness and light and all other attributes desirable to a youthful romanticist, comes out gloriously victorious.

III

The songs.

Throughout Schumann's life his method of composition continued much the same. It was his habit to devote his attention to one form of music at a time and say what he had to say in that medium before passing on to another. The decade 1830-1840 was devoted to piano music. The year 1840 saw the culmination of his troubled and romantic courtship of Clara Wieck, and with their marriage began that lyric outpouring of his soul which has given us some of the most beautiful songs in all musical literature. In February of that year he writes: "Since yesterday morning I have written about twenty-seven pages of music (something new) and I can tell you nothing more about it, except that I laughed and cried over it with delight." And a few months later: "I have been composing so much that it really seems quite uncanny at times. I cannot help it, and should like to sing myself to death, like a nightingale." Altogether, he composed over one hundred songs in this "Song Year," including such masterpieces as "Die Lotosblume," "Mondnacht," "Frühlingsnacht," "Er, der Herrlichste von Allen," "Ich grolle nicht," and "Die Beiden Grenadiere."

The songs have the same melodic freshness, richness of harmony, subtlety of color and vigor of rhythm that distinguished the piano music, but they show the greater maturity of the composer. They are more direct in utterance, and free from eccentricities of manner and incoherence of structure which marked the earlier works. In comparing them with Schubert's songs we feel at once Schumann's more cultivated literary sense and his greater subjectivity. Because of this he carried the blending of the poem and the music to a still further point than did Schubert, who, although often inspired by the spirit of the verses or of some phrases of them, still too often treated the piano part as an accompaniment. Schumann's training as a pianist and a composer for the piano forbade this, and in his songs the pianoforte holds a position of equality with the voice, and both are used together for expression of the poetic idea.

IV

The New Journal of Music ("Neue Zeitschrift für Musik.")

During all these years Schumann was exemplifying his love for the pure and sincere in art not only in his musical composition but in his published writings. In 1834 he founded the *New Journal of Music,* which had for its object "the elevation of German taste and intellect by German art, whether by pointing to the great models of old time, or by encouraging younger talents," and for ten years he acted as its editor, and for the rest of his life, either by active aid or passive influence, remained its guiding genius. Under his leading it never failed in its vow to encourage young talent. No sincere artist was neglected or snubbed. Indeed the mistake, if mistake it can be called, was in the other direction, and the modern reader can but smile sympathetically at the eager enthusiasm with which it proclaims the advent of long-since-forgotten geniuses. But when, in 1853, Schumann resumed the pen neglected for some years to write in his famous article "New Paths" of the advent of Brahms—"the chosen youth, over whose cradle the Graces and the Heroes seem to have kept watch"—there was no mistake, and one of the world's great composers was redeemed from the heels of the Philistines.

V

The orchestral works.

But this literary work was only a by-product, a sort of running comment on his musical studies. He was all this time continuing his composition, and indeed preparing to attempt more ambitious forms. 1841 saw the production of three symphonies, the B flat major, sometimes called "Spring," the D minor, which was withdrawn and not published until ten years later as number 4 (the C major and the E flat, numbers 2 and 3, having meanwhile appeared), and finally the work eventually known as the Overture, Scherzo, and Finale, opus 52.

A lyrical symphonist.

For several reasons these works, fine as they are, do not hold quite the supreme place in symphonic literature that their author's earlier compositions hold in the literature of the piano. First of all, his genius was lyrical and subjective rather than objective or epic. That is to say, he was happier in the vivid characterization of a personal emotion than in the patient and thoughtful building up of a many-sided conception of musical beauty. In this respect he was a true romanticist. But the type of musical ideas thus natural to him was more suitable for short pieces, and for the intimate atmosphere of a small room, than for the large spaces and the public conditions of the symphony. Often in his symphonic allegros, especially in the development sections, we feel the strain he is under to fill this immense canvas; he repeats wearisomely small phrases, or else stretches an idea beyond its elastic power and makes it flabby. Moreover, the whimsicality that is such a charm in his piano pieces forsakes him when he writes for orchestra—necessarily: for one can indulge a whim when one is seated at the piano, but to be playful with an orchestra is like making a pet of an elephant.

To this fundamental difficulty was added a lack of instinct for the technique of orchestration odd in one with so keen a sense of piano effect as Schumann. He lacked confidence in his ability to get just the one inevitable combination of instruments necessary for each passage, and so resorted to the unfortunate plan of "doubling"—of reinforcing one instrument by another, often with the result that each covers up and annuls the other and that the two orchestral colors, like pigments unskilfully mixed, make gray. "He worked almost always," says Weingartner, "with the full material, and did not take the pains to elaborate the parts according to the character of the separate instruments. . . . Therefore his instrumentation is heavy and inflexible."

Yet a great one.

But perhaps we could not ask for a better evidence of Schumann's great musical gift than that in spite of these drawbacks, in spite of the leaning of his genius to the intimate and the subjective, and in spite of his lack of instinct for the orchestra, there are still pages, even complete movements, in his symphonies, of so noble a conception, of so fresh a beauty, of so deep an expressiveness, that they must unquestionably rank him as a symphonist with Beethoven and Schubert. There is, for instance, the whole *Adagio espressivo* of the Second Symphony, with its broadly planned climax, and the let-down that comes with the

CHAP. III

descending trills of the violins while oboe and clarinet sound the theme below. There is the Bach-like *Sostenuto assai* that opens the same symphony. There are the so-called "Cathedral movement" of the Rhenish, the tender Romance of the D minor, and many fine passages scattered through all four symphonies.

Even more successful are the overtures, especially "Manfred" and "Genoveva," in which Schumann has the advantage of a literary as well as a musical impulse. Weingartner finds in the "wonderfully planned and unusually lofty overture of 'Manfred,' his only piece of orchestral music which can be compared with that he wrote for the pianoforte."

Example for analysis, No. 6, Overture, "Manfred."

The student should become familiar first of all with the two musical themes on which this overture is built, representative of the two chief figures in Byron's poem, the gloomy Manfred and the tender Astarte. The theme of Manfred (measures 25—fourth beat—38), in the sombre tonality of E flat minor,* with its constant syncopations and its never-resting accompaniment figure, is singularly expressive of the agitation and morbid melancholy of the Byronic hero. Contrast with it intensifies the plaintive tenderness of the melody associated with Astarte (measures 52-82). Wholly Schumannesque is the subtle curve of the phrase at measures 54-55, as is also the poig-

*Although this overture is in the key of E♭ minor, Schumann writes the signature as if for E♭ major—three flats, adding accidentals as needed. He may have considered that six flats would look too formidable.

nant "appoggiatura"* which introduces the little group of notes in measure 68 that later plays so important a rôle.

Going back to the beginning now, we find, first, three vigorous syncopated chords, establishing at once the tragic atmosphere, and then a series of quiet preluding harmonies on which supervenes at the sixth measure a suggestion of the Manfred theme. This is briefly developed and leads through increasing agitation to the statement of the complete theme (26-38), the beginning of the "Exposition." The transition (39-51) is brief, and constructed out of the first theme itself. As we have already seen, the main tonality is E flat minor. Now Schumann instinctively felt that the second theme also must be in the minor mode—the nature of the subject demanded sombre coloring throughout. His solution of the structural problem thus raised was to put it in the key of F sharp minor, the tonic of which is enharmonically equivalent to the mediant of his original key. This entire section is rhythmically very fine. Note the contrast of the broad phrase first heard in measure 62 with the incisive vigor of the motive introduced four measures later, and exploited in measures 81-83, 93-95, and especially in the Development, measures 181 *et seq.* The piece as a whole owes much of its indomitable energy to this three-note rhythm. Just at the end of the Exposition (measures 96-103) is a very beauti-

*A melody note foreign to the harmony, but neighbor to a harmonic note.

ful treatment of the Astarte motive with the "appoggiatura," over rising chromatic harmonies of Wagnerian flavor.

This motive is the first one to be taken up in development. A pause full of awe and mystery is occasioned by its alternation, in the bass, (measures 110, 112) with high soft chords (111, 113). The passage marked "Mit grosser Kraft,"* developed from measure 62, is less original, but effective in building up the climax that debouches in the Recapitulation of themes at measure 194.

We may pass from there direct to the coda, forty measures before the final "Langsam," one of Schumann's finest inspirations, orchestrally as happy as it is musically original. The materials are simple. First, the cadence harmonies already heard at the beginning (in measures 2-3), but now sombre, almost threatening, on the trombones. Second, above this persistently reiterated foundation, part of the Astarte melody (from measures 61-63), becoming reduced presently to an undulating figure of great beauty. Third, glimpses of the other Astarte phrase (measures 54, 55) presented now in a pathetic thinness. The undulations slow and quiet down until they are finally exhausted in the "Langsam," and with a few broken suggestions of the main themes the overture ends in shadowy gloom.

*Overtures of Schumann, arranged for piano, two hands. Edition of Breitkopf and Härtel.

VI

Chamber music.

The same limitations which Schumann's training and temperament set to his orchestral writing is felt in his chamber music. In the year 1842 he wrote three string quartets, a piano quartet and a piano quintet. The string quartets, beautiful as they are in places, especially in lyric movements, leave much to be desired in point of style. In his string quartet writing his lack of early technical training is particularly felt, and his special qualities are less salient than elsewhere. But the case is very different when the piano is introduced. Here he is in his element; all his mastery of piano idiom is available, and the piano quintet, for instance, is one of the most delightful and successful of his works. The same can be said of his piano concerto, which is considered by many pianists the most grateful work of its kind in music literature, and which is certainly in his happiest vein.

VII

Later years and summary.

In the later years of Schumann's life he turned his attention largely to choral and operatic music. Among the several cantatas which he wrote "Paradise and the Peri" stands pre-eminent. Here we find his fancy, stimulated more by the general idea of the poem than by Moore's rather second-rate verses, revealing the same suggestive melodic phrases, rich and subtle harmonization and delicate beauty, which is characteristic of the composer's most individual work. In his opera "Genoveva" and in the scenes for the setting of "Faust," we find him generally less successful, though occasionally, as in the scene of Faust's salvation, he reaches a supreme height. On the whole, however, his genius did not seem pre-eminently suited to the dramatic form. He was too subjective to succeed in objectively embodying alien personalities in his music. Too many of the figures in the dramas fail to become living forms. His villains sing like heroes, and his heroines are like marionettes. It was only in the cases where the experiences of the characters were such as Schumann could feel himself that he rises to his greatest heights.

Illness and death.

As early as 1844 Schumann suffered from the first attack of a nervous malady which eventually undermined his health, and after a particularly serious breakdown in 1854 it was necessary to have him cared for in a private asylum near Bonn. Here he lingered in pathetic and increasing melancholy and weakness until July 29, 1856, when he died in the arms of his devoted wife.

In spite of his youthful struggles, the hardships and disappointments of his manhood, and his untimely death, Schumann's fate may well be counted happy. His married life was peculiarly fortunate in the companionship of his heroic and gifted wife, his generous service of his art brought him the reward of an ever-widening circle of appreciative friends as well as increasing prosperity, and his music in spite of the limitations which its very qualities imposed upon it, must rank among that of the great masters. As Mr. Hadow writes in his volume of "Studies in Modern Music": "We can discard some of Schumann's compositions as uninspired, but when we have done so there will still be left a legacy that may enrich music to the end of the world. It matters little whether his monument be large or small, in either case it is imperishable."

CHAPTER IV

Felix Mendelssohn

I

Mendelssohn a Romanticist.

N TIMES of change or advance in art, there is always need of a restraining and conserving force to hold back the impetuous ardor of the reformers, maintain the standard of beauty already won, and gradually educate the mass of the public in the new paths. Such a position of conservatism and conciliation was filled among the romanticists by Mendelssohn, a romanticist by his poetic nature and picturesqueness of fancy, a classicist in his style and technical impulse. Educated in the classical technique, with a natural love for the formal rather than the expressive in beauty, he was, nevertheless, swept into the romantic movement, and became the most prominent exponent of one of its phases. In spite of his conservatism and natural reserve, he responded to the call of his times for the picturesque, the romantically expressive. In the descriptive titles of his pieces ("Ruy

Blas," "Hebrides," "Calm Sea and Prosperous Voyage," etc.), as well as in the imitative nature of some of his themes, he shows his reaction to the new impetus in the artistic life about him. He has been called "a romanticist with a classical equipment." He alone of the leaders of the movement was provided with a thorough musical education. We have seen how inadequate Schubert felt his instruction to be, and how late in life Schumann was able to undertake the study of the technique of his art. Mendelssohn was hampered neither by Schubert's poverty nor Schumann's undiscerning guardians. From his infancy, his genius was fostered by all the means that intelligent affection and ample wealth could suggest.

II

Circumstances of his early life.

Born in Hamburg in 1809, the son of a wealthy Jewish banker, and the grandson of a well-known philosopher and scholar, he grew up in an atmosphere of cultivation which favored the growth of his talent to an extraordinary perfection. With his brothers and sisters, all musically gifted, he shared instruction in the arts and sciences, in sports and dancing, shining among them all, the bright particular star of the constellation. At his father's home in the environs of Berlin, where his youth was passed, he was thrown constantly in the society of the most cultivated spirits of the age. Humboldt, Zelter and Goethe became his friends. In a youthful letter written from Goethe's home in Weimar, he tells of playing the piano to the poet, who sat in the shadow listening "like a Jupiter Tonans, with his old eyes flashing fire."

It was the custom of the Mendelssohn family to give weekly receptions or musicales, in which the children would take part as actors, players or authors. Most of Mendelssohn's early works were written for these social occasions. It was for a party in the garden-house of their ample grounds that Felix wrote in the year 1826 the "Midsummer Night's Dream Overture," a work of inimitable delicacy and charm, reflecting all the freshness and gaiety of his youthful nature, while at the same time showing an absolute command of technical resources.

Early work.

Thanks to the extraordinary thoroughness of his education, as well as to the character of his genius, his work was from the first technically perfect. He had assimilated harmony, counterpoint and fugue as unconsciously as most boys assimilate reading, writing and arithmetic. But more than this, he had already developed a style and individuality of his own. In the protected happiness of his home life no beautiful impulse had been stifled or worthy aspiration denied. There is in these works not the slightest trace of youthful turgidity. On the contrary, one of the most prominent traits is their cool dispassionateness, as of the deliberate, detached artist. Everywhere it reveals itself, in the suavity of his melody, in the purity of his harmony, in the fluency of his part-writing. Violent contrasts, strained dissonances, were foreign to his nature and repugnant to his taste. As a romanticist he felt the need of revealing his ideas in music, but differing in temperament from his contemporary Schumann, he was not subjective, but rather objective, in his method. He did not reveal what he felt and thought of life, but instead he painted a picture of what he saw about him, or what he fancied there might be in a fairy world. Even in these early works, when his youthful spirits were bubbling with happiness and friendly mischief, all his music was written, not to be as expressive of his thoughts and feelings as he could make it, but to be as beautifully suggestive of some outside thing as he could make it. In the "Midsummer Night's Dream Overture" and in the scherzo of the Octet, although both were written when he was hardly more than a boy, his genius found almost perfect expression. The light, whimsical, unreal atmosphere of fairyland was one he could make peculiarly his own. It was only when he attempted to portray the tragedy of the feelings and experiences of real life that he fell short. Then, as for instance in the piano pieces, the "Songs Without Words," we find a tameness, a monotony, almost sentimentality, due partly to technical peculiarities, but primarily to his own individual limitations.

III

Travels.

In 1829, at the beginning of a three years' tour planned by his ever-devoted father as a finish to his education, he made his first visit to England. There he was received with the warm appreciation which he retained all his life. Indeed nowhere, not even in his native land, has his fame been more enduring. Then, and in all subsequent visits, he was met with a warm, sympathetic understanding singularly grateful to his delicately nurtured spirit. From England he went to Scotland, where his poetic imagination was strongly impressed by the wild and beautiful ocean scenery. It was during this journey that he began the "Hebrides Overture," finished ten years later. Continuing his travels through South Germany, Switzerland and Italy, he returned home in 1832 by way of Paris and a second visit to London. It was on his third visit to the latter city, a year later, that his "Italian Symphony" was first performed. To his peculiar genius these travels were of great importance. A more subjective temperament would have found ample food for artistic reaction in its own emotional or mental processes. But Mendelssohn needed and profited by the stimulus of outside suggestion. He painted tone landscapes of what his fancy saw in nature and in fairyland. In the "Hebrides" he shows us the rise and fall of the sea, the flight of birds, the tossing of the spray on the black rocks; in the "Italian Symphony" we see the marching pilgrims under the sunny skies. His art reflected nature as through a clear, unclouded glass.

When Wagner called Mendelssohn "the greatest of landscape painters," he was perhaps thinking of the "Hebrides" Overture. It is a singularly happy combination of the classical methods of structure and thematic development with a romantic sense of "atmosphere" or "local color," and the typical romantic power to evoke almost the bodily sensations one would have in the presence of the scene by its artful suggestion in sound.

Example for analysis, No. 7. Overture, the "Hebrides"

It begins at once, without slow introduction, with the undulating figure suggestive of the ocean. Mendelssohn, who visited Fingal's Cave in the Hebrides Islands when he was twenty, is said to have conceived this idea on the spot, and to have sketched the first sixteen bars of it in a letter home. Both the attractive melodic motive and the accompaniment figures that later uphold it in the low strings certainly have in them the very pulsation of sea-billows. At the long, slow, upward scales of measures 15 and 19 we can almost feel the green roller buoying up our boat. The dynamic changes, too, are wonderfully effective, coming as they do with the unexpectedness and something of the illogicality of nature.

The undulatory motion is gradually transferred to the upper register (violins), and at measure 47 appears in the 'cellos, in the relative major key of D major, the main key being B minor, the highly Mendelssohnian second theme, graceful, if a little effeminate. Later taken up by the violins, it passes into a poising passage (measures 67-69), and thus back to bits of the first theme again, leading now to a stormy climax of the full orchestra (measures 77 *et seq.*), culminating in clarion calls from the brass (measures 93-95).

The development now begins, most suggestively and poetically, with a pianissimo expansion of the chief theme, tried several times tentatively, so to speak, in various keys, and each time interrupted by the call. All this is in the happiest orchestral style. Presently appears a vigorous phrase (measures 112-113), followed by silence, and recurring several times thus with highly dramatic effect. This is a development from the part of the first theme originally heard in measures 7-8. A brief episode founded on the second theme intervenes at measures 123-130, after which the treatment of the main subject is resumed, and presently assumes a light, scherzo-like character (measures 149-167). Once more comes a climax; this time the waves lash themselves into fury, and the long upward chromatic scale in measures 180-182 is like the rush and clash of great billows. The quicker bit of chromatic scale in measure 183 is one of the happiest thoughts in the overture. "There is a place in 'The Hebrides'," says Mr. Cecil Forsyth of it in his "Orchestration," "where the upward rush of the two flutes *after* the *fortissimo* of the rest of the orchestra suggests, in the most picturesque manner, the little crest of spray flung into the air by the huge wave as it breaks. The passage is as simple as it is vivid,—merely an F sharp and a chromatic scale, but as a tiny piece of tone-painting it is quite irresistible."

The juncture with the Recapitulation is also most cleverly handled. The violins continue their slow trill on F sharp, started after this dash of spray, and underneath them the main theme sets in quietly, as at first.

This time the second theme, in B major, is sung by solo clarinet over soft, sustained chords. There is a fairly extended second development or coda, reaching a new climax, but then all quiets down to a most poetic end of plucked strings under a single held flute note.

In conclusion, a comparison once made by the present writer between this overture of Mendelssohn and the "Manfred" of Schumann analyzed in the preceding article, may be quoted here.*

"Schumann's work is intensely human from the opening onslaught of syncopated chords to the final, deep-drawn sighs of the contrabasses. There is unassuagable desire in the melody so appropriately marked "In leidenschaftlichem Tempo," there is the very accent of a lover's longing in the beautiful Astarte theme. The music constantly rushes on into feverish excitement, only to expend

*"The Romantic Composers," by Daniel Gregory Mason, page 177.

Chap. IV

its force and die away to tender sadness whence in a moment it lashes itself again into new fury. From this so human world—

> "'Of infinite passion, and the pain
> Of finite hearts that yearn'—

Mendelssohn transports us, in his 'Hebrides,' to an island set in a boundless expanse of the sea, where we watch only the rise and fall of great billows and hear the long sigh of the wind and the cries of sea-birds. The fierce dissonances of Schumann, his ceaseless modulation, his never-resting movement, give place to clear ethereal harmonies, to high, pure trumpet calls, poising violin melodies, and the thin note of the oboe suggesting infinite distance, and to an undulating movement like the ebb and flow of winds and waves. These two works are typical. If Schumann is incomparable in his insight into the storm and stress of the human heart, Mendelssohn is one of the greatest of landscape painters."

IV

Later years.

For three years after his return to Germany he filled the position of music-director in Düsseldorf, beginning here the work, for which the world owes him so large a debt, of introducing to the public masses by Beethoven and Cherubini, motets by Palestrina, and cantatas by Bach—treasures which might well have been lost forever but for his persevering researches and loving study.

In August, 1835, he accepted an invitation

to go to Leipsic as conductor of the famous Gewandhaus Orchestra, and continued his connection there, in spite of the increasing weight of work as conductor in outside and often distant cities, until 1842, when he went to Berlin as Music-Director-General, living there with his family, in the old home where he had spent his youth. In 1844 and again in 1846 and 1847 he visited London to conduct concerts for the Philharmonic Society and other organizations. He was conducting in Frankfort when the news was brought him of the unexpected death of his favorite sister, "Fanny." At this blow his delicate, nervous organization, already weakened by years of continuous overwork, succumbed entirely. His strength and spirits gradually ebbed, and a few months later (November 4, 1847) he died in Leipsic. The whole town mourned for him. "It is lovely weather here," wrote n English student, "but an awful stillness prevails. We feel as if the king were dead." He was buried in Berlin, near the graves of his sister and parents.

V

Summary.

Mendelssohn's life was throughout what we call a fortunate one. Brought up under the most happy circumstances, always the admired of his circle, happily married, and busily occupied with congenial work, praised on every side and in every capacity, only a man of almost superhuman poise could have withstood the insidious dangers of such circumstances, and even the sweet-natured Mendelssohn was somewhat embittered and limited by them. For it is almost as limiting to know only the comfortable and beautiful side of life as to see only the hard and ugly one. Mendelssohn grew exacting and oversensitive. "The atmosphere of love and appreciation," writes his brother-in-law Devrient, "in which he had been nurtured, was a condition of life to him; to receive his music with coldness was to be his enemy, and he was capable of denying genuine merit in any one who did so. A blunder in manners, or an expression that displeased him, could alienate him altogether."

Superrefinement.

It was only in his art that he could find satisfaction for his over-refined and exacting taste. There he was not hampered by personalities which might unintentionally offend him (as when he was annoyed by what he considered the bad taste of a singer's hair-dressing, and felt obliged to tell her "curls ought never to be black, but light brown or fair"), and could study the works of the masters with the enthusiasm of pure devotion, or depict the beauties of nature in his own compositions by the exercise of his poetic imagination and the elasticity of his perfect technique. His work and his individuality compare with that of most men's as the green-house plant, nourished and fostered by a generous and careful hand, compares with the wild flower of the woods, buffeted by rough winds, coerced by jutting rocks and inhospitable soils, but triumphing with a hardy bloom less perfect, but more vital, than its more pampered brother's.

If, to find Mendelssohn's standing among artists, we apply the test to his music which Matthew Arnold enunciated as the test of great poetry—that it contain "great thoughts greatly expressed"—we must feel that Mendelssohn fell just short of being in the first rank. His manner and method were perfect, but what he had to say lacked a certain vitality and ruggedness which the great masters possess. Mr. Statham, in an excellent article in *The Fortnightly Review* (1895) ends his critique with these words, which seem to sum up the general consensus of opinion as to his place in art: "If, then, we sum up the evidence for and against Mendelssohn's claim to be ranked among the great composers, I think the verdict must be, 'He came very near it.' It is true that from one point of view his record seems too remarkable for such a conclusion. To say that a composer has left the most beautiful and highly finished symphonies and the finest overture ('The Hebrides') since Beethoven, the best violin concerto and the best pianoforte trio since Beethoven, the most popular and effective oratorios since Handel, and the best organ music since Bach—and I think all these propositions can be maintained—seems almost tantamount to calling him a great composer. . . . But still, we cannot but recognize that in comparison with those whose status as 'the great masters' is definitely fixed, Mendelssohn has shortcomings of an important nature which prevent us from ranking him with them."

Example for analysis, No. 8. Fugue in E-minor, Opus 35, No. 1.

Instead of illustrating Mendelssohn's piano music by the "Songs Without Words," nowadays somewhat hackneyed, we may take one of the fugues from the fine set which appeared in 1837, and in which he testified in practice his great reverence for Bach. The fugues are not quite up to the Bach level; Mendelssohn smooths off the corners and softens the dissonances of his polyphony more than his ruggeder, more virile model; but for all that they are among the finest examples of the severe contrapuntal style to be found among romantic compositions.

The plan of the present fugue is somewhat novel. Beginning quietly, Andante espressivo, with a thoughtful theme (Figure III, a),

Figure III.

(*a*) Theme of Mendelssohn's Fugue in E minor, opus 35, No. 1.

(*b*) Inversion of the same theme (key of B minor)

etc.

it increases gradually, but steadily, in agitation, through more than two sections, at the end of which (measure 41) enters an *inversion* of the same theme. This in turn goes through an increasingly strenuous activity, debouching at the height of the long climax into a powerful choral in the old German style (measure 104). A short but beautifully tender coda in the original tempo brings it to an end.

A more detailed analysis is given in the following

TABULAR VIEW

Section I	
Theme in Bass, E minor	Measure 1
Theme in Tenor	" 3
Theme in Alto	" 6
Theme in Soprano	" 8
Theme in Tenor	" 12
Theme in Bass	" 15
Theme in Soprano	" 17
Theme in Tenor	" 19
Section II	
Quiet episode, in relative key (G major)	" 24
Theme in Bass	" 27
Theme in Alto	" 29
Theme in Soprano	" 32
Theme in Tenor (incomplete)	" 36
Section III	
Beginning with a deceptive cadence in the dominant (B minor)	
Theme in Alto, *inverted*	" 41
Theme in Soprano, inverted	" 43
Fragments of inverted theme also heard in	" 46-47
Theme in Bass, inverted	" 48
Pedal point and episodic developments	" 51 seq.
Inverted theme in Soprano	" 62
Episode in climax, made of shorter and shorter fragments of the inverted theme	" 65-72
Debouching into	

Chap. IV

TABULAR VIEW—*Continued*

Section IV

Theme in original form and key, in Soprano	"	73
In Bass	"	77
Pedal point on dominant, with portions of theme in both forms	"	83-91
Theme in Bass	"	91
Choral	"	104-123
Coda, the Theme in E major	"	124-133

CHAPTER V

Berlioz and the Beginnings of Realism

I

IN a town in southeastern France called La Côte St. André was born, December 11, 1803, Hector Berlioz, destined to become the first great representative of a new attitude in music—the dramatic or realistic attitude, as contrasted with the emotional or subjective. His importance in musical history lies not only in the specific value of his own work, distinguished in many respects as is its quality, but in the fact that the systematic exploitation of his idea has given us Programme Music, developed by Liszt, Richard Strauss, and others.

Influence of circumstances on Berlioz's genius.

The originality of Berlioz's musical outlook may have been fostered in some degree by the influences of his environment. Neither his father nor his mother appears to have had much interest in his musical genius. There were few musical instruments in the little town where he spent his youth—a few harps and guitars, and we hear of one piano; no music teachers at all until his father joined with other parents in importing a violinist from Lyons. But although his parents were willing enough that he should learn music as a pastime or accomplishment, they were far from agreeing that he should study it as a serious pursuit, deprecating and deploring his absorption in his art and eventually refusing any countenance to his plans. As a consequence of the lack of sympathy at home and the lack of understanding which he later encountered among the academic teachers in Paris, his musical education was won at the expense of his isolation from all those to whom he might most naturally have looked for encouragement. It is not surprising that his technical training was hardly adequate to the demands which his genius made upon it. Of his musical equipment when he arrived in Paris in 1821 he writes later: "I had never yet set foot in a theatre; all I knew of instrumental music was the quartets of Pleyel, with which the four amateurs composing the Philharmonic Society of my native town used to regale me each Sunday after Mass; and I had no other idea of dramatic music than what I had been able to get in running through a collection of old operatic airs arranged with an accompaniment for the guitar." Yet in the loneliness of his country home he had been writing music since his early boyhood, music far from faultless technically, but containing the germs of many of his later works.

Even after he went to Paris his musical edu-

Desultory education.

cation was of a very desultory order. For a while he ostensibly pursued his studies in medicine, but soon, with characteristic courage, or foolhardiness, as his family considered it, he renounced all intention of following the medical profession, which promised him a comfortable livelihood, and decided definitely to devote himself to music at the cost of forfeiting assistance from his parents. He became a pupil of Lesueur's in harmony, and spent his spare moments in studying Gluck's operas in the library. In 1823 he entered the Conservatory as a regular student; but a more irregular student never scandalized the pedants. He had already formed opinions contrary to theirs on every subject on which they attempted to enlighten him, and made no attempt to disguise his convictions. He worked with relentless energy, but following methods of his own all more or less antagonistic to those of his instructors. Year after year he entered the lists for the Prix de Rome, a prize which would have assured him a comfortable annuity for a period of years, given him the benefit of travel and the opportunity for composition; and each year he failed to win it either because of the startling originality of his ideas, his impolitic behavior, or the stupidity of the judges. It was only on the fifth attempt that by deliberately writing down to the dryest scholastic conventions he got the prize and was free to leave for Rome and work out his ideas in composition.

CHAP. V

Peculiarities of temperament.

II

It is not surprising that Cherubini and the other musicians of the classical school failed to understand what this young iconoclast was driving at. To them, music was something apart from life, at its best, a refuge from life in beauty; to Berlioz, it was a dramatized expression of life. All art was to him the expression of the great romantic adventure—life. Nothing was too trivial, too personal, to be expressed. He continually saw himself as the actor in a play. He conceived life theatrically, with what Mr. Bernard Shaw calls the "Romantic Imagination," or the power to imagine things as they are not. All his youth was spent in a gorgeous land of make-believe. And these imaginings were the themes of his compositions. He fell in love with an Irish actress, Henriette Smithson, and before he had exchanged ten words with her was writing a symphony on the imaginary anguish of a lover in his plight, and, by the sheer fantastic force of his extraordinary energy, getting it performed in the hope of melting her heart. In accordance with his temperament, all his experiences were dramatized or pictured in his music, rather than expressed emotionally. The "Symphonie Fantastique," mentioned above, though an early work, is typical in this respect. Goaded by his passion for his Ophelia, he conceives "a young musician of unhealthily sensitive nature" who "has poisoned himself with opium in a paroxysm of love-sick despair," and he sets forth his hero's adventures in five movements of detailed particularity. He is tormented by jealousy, he is consoled by religion, he walks in the country and listens to the shepherds' songs, he dreams he has murdered his loved one, he is surrounded by witches, his mistress has become a witch herself, the *Dies Iræ* sounds, the guillotine descends—and all is over. Such is the programme of the "Symphonie Fantastique."

Realistic ideals of expressions.

If we compare this work, which was first performed in Paris in 1832, with such a typical example of the romantic school as Schumann's "Manfred" Overture, we shall find that they differ radically in two important respects. In the first place, they aim at different kinds of expression. The romantic type tries, above all, to express emotions; the programmistic or realistic type of Berlioz aims rather at telling a story. One deals with inward feelings, the other with outward happenings; one aims at depth and poignancy, the other at brilliancy and vividness; in a word, one is subjective, the other objective. In thus giving a new turn to musical expression, Berlioz, led by his dramatic temperament to innovations that he could never have evolved by thinking, laid the foundations of modern Programme Music.

Realistic types of structure.

The other respect in which his type of art differs from the romantic one is in the constructive methods it adopted. As we have seen throughout our study of the classical period,* the structural types which evolved during that period, of which the sonata form is the archetype, were based on the threefold process of thematic exposition, development, and restatement. Development was necessitated by the natural tendency of musical ideas to grow, as well as by the need of contrast to prevent monotony. Restatement was necessitated by the natural desire for final unity and completeness of impression. Now neither of these processes are so congenial to realistic music as they are to classical and romantic. So long as a musical theme is associated with an emotion it naturally and necessarily develops, as the emotion itself grows and changes. But when it is associated rather with people, so that each theme or *leit-motiv* is, so to speak, a label, then it is less likely to develop. Moreover, development presupposes a sort of logic, the logic of emotion if not the logic of thought, and Berlioz's mind was certainly more distinguished by its brilliancy than by its sequaciousness. "The dominant qualities of my music," he himself says, "are passionate expression, internal fire, rhythmic animation, and unexpected changes." Thematic development, then, the very essence of the classic sonata, was congenial neither to Berlioz's type of art nor to his personal temperament.

Still less room had the realistic scheme for restatements of themes, such as play so important a part in the sonata. Its first princi-

*See "The Appreciation of Music," by Surette and Mason.

FIGURE IVa.

CHAP. V

f

(pizz.)

FIGURE IVb.

Adagio.
(Flute and Oboe.)

p espressivo.

FIGURE IVc.

ple was obedient subordination of the music to the train of events depicted, to the "story." And the story, of course, never repeated itself, since nothing ever happened twice. Consequently repetition could not be accepted as a constructive principle; if it occurred it was either an accident or the survival of an old convention. Berlioz was too good a musician to reject it altogether (for music without repetition is almost as bad as architecture without symmetry), but he does not treat it as any longer the essential principle of unity, but substitutes for it the free play of *leit-motive,* as in the Wagnerian music-drama.

Example for analysis, No. 9. The Symphonie Fantastique.

Although an early work, the Symphonie Fantastique is as true a "sample" of the stuff of which Berlioz's music is made as we could find. It is based, musically, on one motive, that known as the Fixed Idea ("l'Idée fixe"), and symbolizing the dramatic center of the work, i.e., the hero's idea of the beloved. This melody (Figure IV, a), written when the composer was only twelve years old and incorporated in the symphony seventeen years later, is intensely characteristic of him in its spasmodic manner, its unexpected turns, the detached and jerky style of harmonization, and in its free sweep of rhythm—which always remained one of his finest qualities. The most peculiar thing about it, however, is that so little is done with it in the course of the symphony. A detailed analysis is for that reason hardly worth while. The reason is that Berlioz is thinking of its dramatic meaning rather than its musical suggestion. When, in the ball scene, the hero, in the midst of the gaiety, thinks of the beloved, we hear two phrases of it, pianissimo, from the clarinet—not developed, but precisely as in the first movement. In the third movement, "In the Country," it is treated with rather more interest, taking on the form shown at Figure IV, b. In the "Procession to the Stake" it is used just before the axe falls on the neck of the hero, ending life and the thought of the beloved together—and here the *naïveté* of the realism seems almost childish to any one less capable of "making believe" than Berlioz. The only real development of the motive occurs in the last movement, when it is parodied to represent the beloved in the horrid embodiment of a witch. This is ingenious and effective (see Figure IV, c).

III

The limitations of a pioneer.

As Berlioz himself uses them, then, these new methods seem hardly convincing; it was their possibilities in the hands of more skilled musicians that were important. His results were early and on the whole justly criticized by Wagner. It must be remembered that the Frenchman's use of *leit-motive* is not to be confused with Wagner's "music associated with action," which is not, strictly speaking, music, but a new art, to which its creator gave the name of "music-drama" and which appeals not only to the ear through sounds, but to the eye through scenery and actors, and to the understanding through language. It is quite a different thing to use the same methods in a symphony to be performed by musicians in their ordinary costumes in a concert-room. That Wagner was well aware of the difference is shown by a passage in his essay on Liszt's Symphonic Poems, where he writes: "Whilst listening to the best of this sort (programme music) . . . it had always happened that I so completely lost the musical thread that by no manner of exertion could I refind and knit it up again. This occurred to me quite recently with the love scene, so entrancing in its principal motives, of our friend Berlioz's "Romeo and Juliet" Symphony; the great fascination which had come over me during the development of the chief motive was dispelled in the further course of the movement, and sobered down to an undeniable *malaise;* I discovered at once that, while I had lost the

Wagner's criticism.

CHAP. V

musical thread (i.e., the logical and lucid play of definite motives), I now had to hold on to scenic motives not present before my eyes, nor even so much as indicated in the programme."

It is exactly in this loss of the musical thread, lack of the "logical and lucid play of definite motives," that we find the greatest weakness of this type of music. In Berlioz's case this was further emphasized by the "jerkiness" of his ideas, the unsequaciousness of his harmonies, and his failure to develop his themes even to the extent possible under the limitations of the musical scheme.

IV

Salient qualities.

On the other hand, his rhythmic effects were endlessly varied and interesting. Though Mr. Hadow is just in saying that "time after time he ruins his cause by subordinating beauty to emphasis," and that "he is so anxious to impress that he forgets how to charm," he is equally discriminating when he adds: "His sense of rhythm was, at the time he lived, without parallel in the history of music. It is thanks to the elasticity of his rhythms that Berlioz's music never, like that of most of the Romantic composers, appears to be composed in blocks or sections." The reader will remember that we pointed out how Schumann, for example, too often made up the developments of his symphonic allegros by repeating such short blocks of tune. Schumann is hardly more superior to Berlioz in depth of expressiveness than Berlioz is to him in rhythmic variety.

A master of the orchestra.

Even more than for his rhythmic sense Berlioz is conspicuous among his contemporaries for his unerring instinct for the capacities of the orchestra. As an orchestral colorist he has perhaps never been excelled. Even here, to be sure, he was sometimes betrayed by his extravagance, his love of the sensational and the theatrically effective. He scored his Requiem for sixteen trombones, sixteen trumpets, five ophicleides, twelve horns, eight pairs of kettle-drums, two bass-drums and a gong, in addition to the usual resources. He liked to have horns played in bags, cymbals struck with a stick, drumsticks covered with sponge, and he ventured once on a duet for piccolo and bass trombone. All this cult for mere quantity and for queerness has been only too industriously imitated by the moderns, but it is not Berlioz's real title to be considered a master of the orchestra. That rests, in the first place, on his surprisingly keen instinct for the possibilities of each instrument alone. To his mind a theme seems never to be simply a theme in the abstract, an unembodied musical idea, but a violin melody, a clarinet melody, or a piccolo tune. He conceived shape and color in one act. Secondly, he combined his colors with equal felicity, because with equal vividness of imagination and with complete independence of traditional methods. It has been truly remarked that his scores look different from others. In particular there are

Chap. V

more "rests" in them. This is important, for it means omission, and omission is the reverse side of that selection which is the essence of art. There are no dead notes in Berlioz's scores, everything tells. Doubtless to a taste formed on German models his combinations are sometimes a little thin, but they are thoroughly vital, and free from surplusage and "filling." Mr. Hadow classes him with Beethoven, Wagner and Dvorák as "one of the four greatest masters of instrumentation the world has ever seen."

V

Berlioz's chief works and later life.

Like Mendelssohn, Berlioz wrote his most characteristic work in early life. Nothing that he did later was perhaps more significant than the "Symphonie Fantastique," where his idea of the *leit-motiv* applied to persons and scenes was so fully presented, his grotesque fancy had full play, and his instinct for rhythm and tone-color shone supremely. Later he further exemplified his theories, perhaps a little restrained eventually as he grew older and failing health robbed him of his exuberance of spirits, in his symphony "Romeo and Juliet," the overtures "King Lear," "Benvenuto Cellini" and the "Corsair," the two operas "Beatrice and Benedict" and "The Trojans at Carthage," the "Requiem," and "The Damnation of Faust."

His life was a checkered one, strangely twisted by the combination of an affectionate nature—witness his devotion to his son, his lifelong friendship with his wife even after they had separated—and his fantastic passion for the theatrical, which made him at times an intolerable companion. After several years of apparently happy though poverty-stricken life with the woman he had so tempestuously wooed, he formed a *liaison* with a second-rate singer, and immediately after his wife's death married her. To her, as to his former wife and son, he was devoted, working indefatigably at the newspaper writing which he did so well and hated so fiercely, by way of insuring their support and comfort. As he approached middle life his health gradually failed, and during his later years he was obliged to resort to narcotics to endure the neuralgic pains which tortured him. His life was embittered by the coldness of the Parisian audiences, who remained indifferent when he was received enthusiastically at all the courts of Europe and in England. It was only after his death that Paris acclaimed him as France's greatest musician. He died March 8, 1869.

Summary.

Few composers of any period could make with as much truth as he the proud statement we find in Berlioz's "Autobiography": "The love of money has never allied itself in a single instance with my love of art. I have always been ready to make all sorts of sacrifices to go in search of the beautiful, and insure myself against contact with those paltry platitudes which are crowned by popularity."

As to his standing as a musician there will always be extreme divergence of opinion, so uncompromising was his theory of art, and so relentless his execution of it. Whether so extreme a realism as his is justified by the nature of music will always remain a debated question. But no one can deny the greatness of his incidental service to his art in breaking the narrow bonds of conservatism with which it was confined, and opening up new possibilities in the form and texture of music. Whether his particular ideas shall form a permanent contribution to musical art or not, his place as a contributor to the unceasing progress of art is secure.

CHAPTER VI

Franz Liszt

I

ROM time to time there appears before the public eye a personality so magnetic, so unconsciously persuasive, that he draws men to him by an almost uncanny power, fascinating them until they see in him something superhuman and beyond the pale of their judgment. Such a personality was Franz Liszt, a sort of Pied Piper of men. From his first appearance in public, at the age of nine, when one of his critics pronounced his playing to "border on the miraculous," to his last performances in concert as an old man, there was something almost necromantic in the art with which he held his hearers spellbound. Not only were impressionable women his adoring slaves—supposedly commonplace men were equally dazed by his personal glamour; few, indeed, of either sex were sufficiently cautious and discriminating to judge him dispassionately.

Liszt's early development.

Born in Raiding, a small town in Hungary. October 22, 1811, the only child of Adam

CHAP. VI

Liszt, an officer in the Imperial Service, and of Anna Lager, a German, he early showed his extraordinary talent for music. His father was his first teacher, but by his tenth year it was evident he needed more advanced instruction, and his family moved to Vienna that he might study under the celebrated teachers Czerny and Salieri. The story of his meeting with Czerny shows him at that early age exercising his blandishments. Czerny at first refused to teach him, saying his hours were already overcrowded; whereupon, all uninvited, young Liszt sat down at the piano and proceeded to play, with the result that he was accepted as a pupil without further ado. His progress was remarkable under his new instructors, and in April, 1823, he appeared in public before a highly appreciative audience. It is said that Beethoven was present at the concert and testified his approval by kissing the young player on the forehead. The same year he went to Paris, and, still continuing his studies under Reicher, began his extraordinary career as a virtuoso pianist. The following spring he made a tour in England, where he received the compliments and adulation which had already become his accustomed atmosphere.

As he reached adolescence, however, the studious and intellectual side of Liszt revolted against these comparatively easy triumphs. His pride suffered at the indignity of being advertised as younger than he was, carried on the stage in his manager's arms, and in general treated more like an infant prodigy than a serious artist. He grew melancholy, and already cherished the idea, to which he reverted in later years, of withdrawing from the world into monastic life. "I would rather be anything in the world," he cried, "than a musician in the pay of great folk, patronized and paid by them like a conjurer or the clever dog Munito."

II

Life in Paris.

His prospects were suddenly changed, however, by the death, in August, 1827, of his father, who had attended to all the practical details of his tours. Liszt's concerts were immediately discontinued, and he and his mother returned to Paris. Here he settled down to a life of study and teaching, entering with all his intellectual ardor into the extraordinarily complex life of the French capital. "My mind and fingers have been working like two lost spirits," he writes in 1832; "Homer, the Bible, Plato, Locke, Byron, Hugo, Lamartine, Chateaubriand, Beethoven, Bach, Hummel, Mozart, Weber, are all around me. I study them, meditate on them, devour them with fury; besides this I practice four to five hours of exercises. . . . Ah! provided I don't go mad, you will find an artist in me!"

Love affairs.

Among the leaders of the Romanticism which pervaded artistic life in Paris, as everywhere else in Europe at the time, was the beautiful and fascinating, but vain and am-

CHAP. VI

bitious, Countess d'Agoult, who, under the pseudonym of Daniel Stern, was the author of several novels of contemporary fame. Liszt quickly fell under the spell of her beauty, and entered into a semi-flirtatious, semi-sincere love affair with her, for which, according to some of his biographers, he was obliged to pay dear. After the connection had lasted some months Liszt was ready to bring the affair to an end, but, finding this impossible, he accepted the situation with what grace he could, and entered upon a period of travel with the countess which lasted ten years. Three children resulted from this union, Daniel, Blandine and Cosima. The latter became the wife of Von Bülow, and later of Wagner.

This experience of disillusion doubtless added to the naturally ironical bent of his mind and accounted in part for the cynicism which occasionally appeared in his words and writings. "Women do not believe in a passion which avoids notoriety," quotes his biographer Janka Wohl; and, again, "Misunderstood women are generally women who have been too well understood." Madame Moscheles writes in her reminiscences of Liszt: "His high-flying notions are made more interesting by all the arts of dialectics; but there is a good deal of satire in them, and that satire is like an ill-tuned chord in conversation."

The virtuoso.

It is said that Liszt was prompted to resume his career as a virtuoso by hearing the extraordinary feats of technique which Paganini, the magician of the violin, produced on his instrument. Liszt desired to attain equally marvelous effects of light and shade on the piano. That he was successful in this is proved by contemporary criticism. All Europe was enraptured with his playing. It was described as "art with a soul." Mendelssohn wrote that he had never before seen a musician "so thoroughly imbued with music." Only the few, the most discriminating, like Schumann, who wrote Clara Wieck, "How extraordinary his playing is, so bold and daring, and then again so tender and delicate! . . . but there is a good deal of tinsel about it, too," could see the meretricious element which was hidden in it. With all his unquestioned power and ability, there is no doubt he "played to the gallery." Indeed, he made no secret of his theatric methods to his pupils, saying, for instance, "After you make a run you must wait a minute before you strike the chords, as if in admiration of your own performance. You must pause as if to say, 'How well I did that.'" It was partly due to these methods that he became the most famous virtuoso of his time, but his artistry was founded on other and quite different qualities. There must have been solid merit, indeed, in playing which commanded the homage of all Europe during the eight years, from 1839 to 1847, of his most important work as a concert pianist. "Money, which he prized little," says Hueffer, "the friendship of

Chap. VI

princes and artists and men of genius, and the love of women, which he prized much, poured in on him in one uninterrupted current." No wonder that he was tempted to forget the stern impersonality which the highest art demands.

III

Life in Weimar.

With the year 1847 another period of his remarkable career unfolded. Accepting the position of court music-director in Weimar, the capital of Thuringia, he began a life of most vigorous and many-sided activity, of which the chief phases were conducting, teaching, writing and composing. His connection with the Countess d'Agoult had ceased some time before, and he had formed a "platonic friendship" with the Princess Sayn-Wittgenstein, a woman of strong personality and intense religious sentiments. During the fourteen years of Liszt's stay in Weimar the Princess lived with her daughter in the second floor of his house and acted as his secretary, councillor and muse. As she was not able to secure the pope's permission to divorce her husband she never married Liszt, but their friendship continued until his death.

Conductor and teacher.

As a conductor and teacher Liszt exercised an enormous influence over the music of his time. His intellectual veracity and generosity of heart prompted him to do all in his power, by writing and production, to make known the works of less famous, though in many cases greater, composers than himself. He was one of the first to produce the works of Berlioz, Schumann, Raff, Cornelius, and, above all, Wagner, for whom he labored indefatigably during the long years when Europe refused to listen to his works. He was also one of the prime movers in the establishment of the Festivals at Bayreuth for the regular performance of Wagner's music-dramas.

As a teacher his influence was felt everywhere among pianists. Only Chopin and possibly Schumann can be said to have left so deep an impress on modern pianoforte style. His pupils came from all over Europe and America, and through them the fundamental principles of his art became widely disseminated and reëmbodied.

Liszt the composer.

Probably no music produced in his day, save only Wagner's, has aroused so much controversy, or been the subject of such opposite judgments, as Liszt's. Some critics pronounce it absolutely artificial, theatrical, and insincere; others find in it the most important creation of instrumental music in the nineteenth century, and profess to find foreshadowed in it much of Wagner as well. What is the reason of these extreme differences of estimate?

Theatrical qualities.

Perhaps temperamental leanings have something to do with them. Those who care, above all in music, for a sincere, simple, and eloquent expression of subjective emotion, such as we find, for example, in Bach, in Beethoven, or in Schumann, are doomed to be disappointed in Liszt, because they are not in sympathy with his aims. For them his

CHAP. VI

heroism is bombast, his tenderness mawkish sentimentality.* His everlasting posturing is so distasteful to them that they cannot do justice to the intellectual force which was linked in his strange make-up with this emotional shoddiness. Yet, if we can once admit and tolerate the theatricality of all Liszt's expression, postulating it as essential to his whole conception of art, we shall find in that art much to admire. He was not a subjective, but an objective, musician; he was aiming not at self-expression, but at effect; and he carried the objective, external type of music—programme music—a long step forward.

Innovations in structure.

The fundamental defect of Berlioz's experiments was that, discarding the classical musical forms, he had yet no means of securing coherence and clear organization to substitute for them. His music was, therefore, wandering and fragmentary. Liszt, with his keen analytic intelligence, realized that some definite plan of thematic statement and development was indispensable, and with his thorough technical education and vigorous musical imagination found the means at hand for attaining it. The "symphonic poem"—a type that musical art owes to him—was in essence his solution of the problem of obtaining musical coherence and unity without sacrificing dramatic elasticity. His scheme was to build on two or three generating motives as many sections as were required by the pro-

*See the present writer's essay on Liszt in "The Romantic Composers," pages 333-337.

gramme, the expressive quality of the themes being modified from time to time as the programme might require. Thus musical unity, coherence, interest were maintained by the retention throughout of the generating motives —however transformed they might become— and by using related keys for the various sections. At the same time, the number and order of the sections was determined entirely by the programme, which thus elaborated itself in complete freedom from the restrictions of the older forms.

The symphonic poem.

This dramatico-musical form, as it was worked out by Liszt in his thirteen symphonic poems, of which well-known examples are "Tasso," "Les Preludes," and "Mazeppa," in his Episodes from Lenau's "Faust," and more elaborately in his symphonies on "Faust" and on "The Divine Comedy," has proved itself admirably adapted to the requirements of realistic music, and has been taken up by Saint-Saëns, Tschaikowsky, César Franck, Richard Strauss, and many others. Indeed, our century might almost be called the century of the symphonic poem, just as the nineteenth was the century of the symphony and the eighteenth the century of the suite. Its characteristic methods will become clear in illustration.

*Example for analysis, No. 10. Symphonic Poem, "Les Preludes."**

The programme of "Les Préludes" is from the "Meditations poétiques" of Lamartine:

"What is life but a series of preludes to that

*Breitkopf and Härtel edition. Arrangement for piano, two hands.

unknown song whose initial solemn note is tolled by Death? The enchanted dawn of every life is love; but where is the destiny on whose first delicious joys some storm does not break?—a storm whose deadly blast disperses youth's illusions, whose fatal bolt consumes its altar. And what soul thus cruelly bruised, when the tempest rolls away, seeks not to rest its memories in the pleasant calm of rural life? Yet, man allows himself not long to taste the kindly quiet which first attracted him to Nature's lap; but when the trumpet gives the signal he hastens to danger's post, whatever be the fight which draws him to its lists, that in the strife he may once more regain full knowledge of himself and all his strength."

The music naturally divides itself into six sections: Introduction, Love, Storm, Country Life, War, Conclusion. There are two generating motives, x and y, shown in themes a and b in Figure V. The student will note the x consists of one step downward followed by an upward jump, while the essence of y is the descent to the neighboring note and return to the point of departure.

Figure V.

Section I. Introduction. Motive x is suggested in the passage for strings and in the wood-wind chords, and is slightly developed. With the Andante maestoso (a good example of Liszt's bombast, by the way) it appears in the brass, with an elaborate accompanying figure-work above. In the soft 9-8 section (L'istesso tempo) it is sounded soulfully, not to say unctuously (the two terms are almost synonymous with Liszt), by the violoncellos. It also gives rise to the bass figure which ingeniously punctuates each phrase.

With the entrance of motive y in the four horns the Love section begins. As this progresses both motives are heard and conjointly developed. Especially to be noted is the form of (y) in this rhythm: ♩‿♪.♬ ♫

Section III, Storm, begins with motive x in the bass and with the chromatic scurrying and harmonization in diminished seventh chords that might be expected. The theatrical quality of the music is here obvious enough: we feel that the villain must be just round the corner.

The Allegretto pastorale, A major, 6-8, initiates the Country Life section, musically the most genuine and attractive of all. In the fifteenth measure the student will note the art-concealing art with which Liszt knows how to use his material (motive x). Further on the pastoral theme is combined with motive (y).

Section V, Allegro marziale animato, introduces a martial variant of (x) on the heavy brass and develops a sounding climax, after

CHAP. VI

which the Andante maestoso of the Introduction returns, forming a Conclusion for the work.

IV

Later years.

Liszt's support of comparatively unknown artists naturally aroused criticism among the less appreciative of his audiences and petty-minded musicians. Matters came to a crisis over his production of Cornelius' opera, "The Barber of Bagdad," in 1861, and he resigned from his position as court director. He still continued to pass several months of each year in Weimar, where he had a house presented to him by the Grand Duke, but he had no official position. About this time, however, his mind reverted to the mysticism of his early youth, he went to Rome, entered one of the lower orders of the Church which, fortunately, entailed no ecclesiastical duties, so that he was still able to continue his musical activities, and for seven years lived in great retirement at the monastery of Monte Mario composing constantly, but only sacred music, masses and oratorios. After 1868 this scheme of things changed once more, and from then on his remaining years were spent in a sort of glorious triumphal procession, from Rome to Weimar and from Weimar to Pesth. At Monte Mario he had been the Abbé, now he became "The Master." Amy Fay, in her book called "Music Studies in Germany," gives a vivid description of him at this time. She says: "He is the most interesting and striking man imaginable, tall and slight, with deep-set eyes, shaggy eyebrows, and iron-gray hair. He wears a long abbé's coat, reaching nearly to his feet. His mouth turns up at the corners, which gives, when he smiles, a most crafty and Mephistophelean expression. His hands are very narrow, with long, slender fingers, which look as if they had twice as many joints as other people's. They are so flexible and supple it makes you nervous to look at them. . . . His variety of expression is wonderful. One moment his face will look dreamy, shadowy, tragic, the next insinuating, amiable, ironic, sarcastic. All Weimar adores him. When he goes out every one greets him as if he were a king."

It was in the midst of this halo of praise and sympathetic adulation, while attending one of the performances at the Bayreuth Festival, a performance which could never have existed but for him, that he died, after a brief illness, July 31, 1886, leaving behind him hosts of friends and admirers, the echoes of whose praises are but now dying in our ears.

CHAPTER VII

Frédéric Chopin

I

RÉDÉRIC CHOPIN, born March 1, 1809, in Zelazowa Wola, a small village near Warsaw in Poland, was the third child and only son of Nicholas Chopin, a French émigré, and his Polish wife, Justina Kryzowska. At the time of his son's birth Nicholas was serving as private tutor in the family of the Countess Skarbek, but the following year he accepted a position as professor of French in the Warsaw Lyceum and moved with his family to the capital. For a few years the conditions of life must have been difficult. Napoleon was at the height of his career and no one knew where his armies would strike next. In 1814, however, the Congress of Vienna brought about a more settled condition of things. The Kingdom of Poland was established under the suzerainty of Russia, and the national life began to recover some of its lost prosperity. Nicholas Chopin was put at the head of a private preparatory school. From

Early life.

CHAP. VII

now on the family prospered. Distinguished visitors came to the city and were introduced into their circle. Poets, musicians, scholars and statesmen frequented their home. Except in the Mendelssohn household, nowhere do we find more congenial surroundings for an artist's youth than these which young Chopin enjoyed.

Like the Mendelssohn family, the Chopin children were all talented, and were constantly getting up festivals, plays and concerts for the entertainment of their elders. Frédéric, who was an accomplished pianist at eight and a composer almost as early, took a prominent place in these family parties. At the same time he had begun playing in public, sometimes before the Grand Duke, and even, a little later, before the Emperor Alexander himself, who was so pleased with the young artist that he presented him with a diamond ring.

But in spite of his extraordinary precocity and the praise which was heaped upon him, Chopin was then, and always continued to be, singularly free from vanity, seeing clearly that, however much he might seem to outsiders to have accomplished, he was still far below the standard of excellence which his own genius set as his ideal.

A true artist.

During his boyhood and youth we read much of his sunny, playful, sensitive temperament. His health was not robust, and he was not fond of boisterous sports or long walks, but he was not ill or morbid, and was re-

Chap. VII

markable for a "sparkling effervescence that manifested itself in all sorts of fun and mischief." He could laugh at himself and at his own lack of physical prowess; as when he wrote one of his boy friends saying that he let his horse go where it pleased, sitting on it, like a monkey, with fear, and that in driving he always took a back seat for safety.

His teachers in music were Zywny in piano playing and Elsner in theory and counterpoint. We find little evidence of their capabilities as musicians, but they both seem to have had an intuition of the method to pursue with the sensitive genius entrusted to them, and left it to develop naturally with as little coercion from them as possible. As a result, although Chopin never became a master of counterpoint or of the larger forms of musical composition, he worked out for himself, in a limited field, a peculiarly perfect musical expression. It is quite possible that had he been left in the control of more technically competent but less imaginatively sympathetic instructors the genius which flowed in his incomparable art might have been smothered under the formalism of classic rules.

In 1828 Chopin visited Berlin, and we read in his letters of his seeing Mendelssohn and Spontini, and of his shame at mistaking the great Alexander von Humboldt for a footman. The next year he spent two months in Vienna, where he gave his first foreign concert and was showered with praise and compliments as he was wont to be in Warsaw.

II

Life in Paris.

But it was not until his arrival in Paris in 1831, which was to be his home for the rest of his short life, that his independent artistic life began. Until then his work had been tentative, a docile imitation of the masters until he should learn for himself the language in which they spoke. Only now did he show himself a finished virtuoso and a mature artist.

It had originally been his intention to continue his studies under some famous master in Paris. He therefore went immediately on his arrival to see the great teacher Kalkbrenner. It is characteristic of the young artist's modesty that although Kalkbrenner made the almost prohibitive stipulation that the lessons must continue for three years Chopin seriously considered the proposal, and only decided against it on the advice of his old teacher Elsner.

Early in 1832 he made his début before a Parisian audience in a concert in aid of the Polish refugees. He was immediately recognized as a unique genius among the musicians, and his position was at once established in artistic circles. "Evening after evening," says Mr. Hadow, "was occupied with visitors or filled with invitations; pupils began to present themselves; concert managers solicited his services, and before long he shared with Liszt the honor of being the most fashionable musician of the day." It speaks well for his wisdom that all this neither confused nor unduly elated him. "If I were more silly than I am," he wrote, "I might imagine myself a finished artist; but I feel daily how much I have still to learn." In spite of the temptation to lead the life of a virtuoso and earn easily both praise and money, he settled down to the drudgery of teaching and study, and soon the appearance of some of his most characteristic compositions justified his decision.

Method of work.

Heretofore his compositions though personal enough in inspiration had been somewhat conventional in form. Even the "Là ci darem la mano" Variations (Op. 2), which had called forth Schumann's enthusiastic "Hats off, gentlemen, a genius!" had not shown that entire mastery of his material which his work now attained in the series of short pieces, mazurkas, waltzes, polonaises, études, preludes and nocturnes where his genius found its characteristic expression.

That the perfection of these veritable gems was no matter of chance, but the result of painstaking labor, is proved by a description of his method of work given some time later by George Sand. "He shut himself up in his room for whole days," she writes, "weeping, walking, breaking his pens, repeating and altering a bar a hundred times, writing and effacing it as many times, and recommencing the next day with a minute and desperate perseverance." And with all his labor he was never satisfied with the result, and always saw what he had striven to express still beyond his powers. The original character of his music, which depends largely for its effect on the penumbra of dissonant tones which he brings to our notice grouped about his melodies, gave him, moreover, a more delicate and nerve-racking problem than that of the less subtle writers of piano music who had preceded him.

Ill health.

In 1836-7 Chopin suffered a severe attack of influenza, a premonition of the pulmonary trouble which eventually brought about his death. A year later, being ordered south by his physician, he made the ill-fated visit to the Island of Majorca with his friend George Sand (Madame Dudevant) and her children, from which he returned permanently broken in health. Hereafter, during the twelve years which remained to him, his life was a constant struggle to accomplish his work under the handicap of increasing bodily weakness and depression of spirits.

Frederick Niecks, at the close of his admirable biography of Chopin, has given us a vivid picture of the artist's curiously dual nature. "Notwithstanding the lack of robustness and all it entails," he says, "Chopin might have been moderately happy if body and soul had been well matched. This, however, was not the case. His thoughts were too big, his passions too violent, for the frail frame that held them; and the former grew bigger and more violent as the latter grew frailer and frailer. He could not realize his aspirations, could not compass his desires, in short, could not fully assert himself. . . . Had not Chopin been an artist the tale of his life would forever have remained a tale untold. But in his art he revealed all his strength and weakness, all his excellences and insufficiencies, all his aspirations and failures, all his successes and disappointments, all his dreams and realities."

He died in Paris October 17, 1849, and was buried in a place of honor among the great French musicians at Père la Chaise.

Chopin a one-instrument composer.

Chopin confined himself to one instrument more than any other great composer. Aside from a small volume of Polish songs, a trio for piano and strings and one or two works for violoncello and piano, and, of course, the orchestral accompaniments of his two concertos, the work of his entire life was for the piano. Such specialization naturally resulted in extraordinary skill; probably no other composer is so absolutely idiomatic to the instrument as Chopin; and, on the other hand, the peculiarities of the piano, its special merits and defects, never dominated a style so completely as they do his. His wonderful shimmering tone-color has rightly been insisted upon as one of his chief glories—and it is the product of sympathetic vibration and clashing over-tones as made possible by the damper pedal of the piano—a device paralleled in no other instrument.

The damper pedal came into general use

only in 1780, when Beethoven was already ten years old. Haydn and Mozart, who formed their piano style without it, abound in those accompaniments of broken chords, for the left hand, in close position, which were called Alberti basses (Figure VI, a). The effect of such accompaniments was always unsatisfactory in one or the other of two ways: either, if the position was comparatively high, as in the example from Mozart, a solid bass was lacking, or, if the position was for that reason made low, as in the example from Beethoven in Figure VI, b, the harmony became thick and the tone-color "muddy." It was only gradually that composers realized that, thanks to the damper pedal, they might make such figures cover a much wider space, beyond the reach of one position of the hand, and thus get a vastly improved sonority. A glance at the way Grieg, in his second piano part of Mozart's sonata, rewrites the left hand part, is most instructive on this point (Figure VI, c). Without a pedal this would be awkward—impossible for small hands; with the help of the pedal it gives a firm bass and full harmony to support the right-hand melody. Chopin is a past master at this kind of accompaniment; his works are a mine of suggestion as to the ways in which the pedal may free the left hand from its old-time shackles; and the student who wishes to see for himself how much invention a real artist will lavish even on minor matters may well examine the left-hand parts of the nocturnes,

FIGURE VI.

(a)
Mozart, Sonata in C major.
Allegro.
tr
(b)
Beethoven, Sonata, opus 7.
etc.
(c)
Grieg, Second Piano to
Mozart's Sonata in C major.
(d)
Chopin, Nocturne No. 1.
etc

the impromptus, and many of the etudes and preludes.

Example for analysis, No. 11. Étude in A flat, opus, 25, No. 1.

In Opus 25, No. 1, we see illustrated the widespread figures that the pedal makes possible, not only in the left hand, but in the right hand as well. This is piano music—music that could not possibly be played on a harpsichord or on an organ. See, for instance, the eleventh measure from the end: in order to pick out that high F the hand has to pass quite out of the register of its accompaniment notes, which can be sustained only by the pedal.

This étude is also an object lesson in the clear distinction that has to be made, in playing Chopin, between what may be called essential notes, and harmony or color notes. The latter, to be run together by a light and *unindividualizing* touch, are here printed in smaller note-heads. The former, giving the essential lines of the composition, are printed in larger heads, and must be played with a singing quality. "Imagine," said Schumann of this étude, "an Æolian harp that had all the scales, and that these were jumbled by the hand of an artist into all sorts of fantastic ornaments, but in such a manner that a deeper fundamental tone and a softly singing higher part were always audible, and you have an approximate idea of his playing."

Chopin's conception of tone-color, guided and enriched by the damper pedal and a habit of intent listening such as few pianists ever attain,* soon came to require, indeed, a special technique, and in particular an ability to subordinate the unimportant, which few players of his day possessed. In a Bach fugue every note is important and must be clearly rendered; in a Chopin nocturne many notes are for color only and must be kept in the background. "The harsh modulations," said Moscheles, a player of the old school, "which strike me disagreeably when I am playing his compositions no longer shock me [when he plays them], because he glides over them in a fairy-like way with his delicate fingers"; and a contemporary describes his touch as "so insinuating and gossamer that the crudest and most chromatic harmonies floated away under his hand, indistinct yet not unpleasing." The steel engraver aims always at distinctness, but the pastel worker has a different standard and often blurs his outlines so that they fade almost imperceptibly into each other. So the player of Chopin, when the conception of the piece demands it, must have the intelligence and courage to merge dozens of notes, by means of an unindividualizing touch and a lavish pedal, into one vague complex of sound. Furthermore, so rapidly has the appetite for rich effects of clashing dissonances grown, under the pampering it

*Mr. Arthur Whiting, in the preface to his "Pianoforte Pedal Studies," imagines what would happen if the dampers were normally away from the strings and brought in contact with them by the pedal: "In this state the listening pianist would be the rule; the player who leaves listening to others, the exception."

has received in recent years, that he will often find even Chopin's pedal markings too reserved for contemporary taste.

Example for analysis, No. 12. Prelude in B flat, opus 28, No. 21.

Opus 28, No. 1 is an especially interesting piece for study from the point of view of subordination of color to line, or distinction of planes, so to speak, into primary and secondary, foreground and background. The melody of the right hand and the single bass notes on the accents are, of course, the essence of the musical idea, and are to receive the clearest delivery. But how about the phrased figures in the left hand? They have a real melodic quality of their own; they are attractive and graceful; they seem to demand loving attention. There can be no doubt, however, that if they are made as prominent as the main melody they detract from rather than enhance its effects. They must be kept in the second plane. To do this, and yet render justice to their intrinsic charm, is a study worth the mettle of any pianist.

We should nowadays keep the pedal through the whole of measures 13 and 14, which are simply dominant harmony richly embroidered, changing only for the tonic chord in measure 15. With properly gradated touch, again, the student will find it possible to keep one pedal from the start of measure 17 to the second beat (inclusive) of measure 32, and the effect so obtained will be more fluid than if the pedal is changed at measures 19 and 25. But the most striking instance is found in the passage from measure 39 to the sec-

CHAP. VII

ond beat of 44, all to be played with one pedal, and beginning fortissimo. It has a barbaric clangor. The harmony changes, and the pedal with it, at the third beat of the latter measure.

III

Chopin as a melodist.

Much as still remains unsaid on the fascinating subject of color in Chopin's music, these notes must not be concluded without at least touching upon another and perhaps deeper aspect of his genius, his power to create noble and beautiful melodies. Melody in music corresponds in a general way to line in the plastic arts, and as no colorist can take first rank unless his drawing is also correct, imaginative, and powerful, so no composer is really of the first order unless he be a noble melodist. The admiration that all serious musicians feel for Chopin, to say nothing of his immense popularity with the public, shows that he is one of these really great melodists—indeed, he is one of the greatest. Mr. James Huneker has devoted his book, "The Greater Chopin," to a discussion of the heroic aspect of the master whose more delicate qualities have been perhaps overemphasized by critics. The student may be referred to that book, and to such studies as Mr. W. H. Hadow's, in his "Studies of Modern Music," and to Mr. Edgar Stillman Kelley's recently published "Chopin the Composer." Above all, he should analyze, phrase by phrase, the themes of the nocturnes, the polonaises, the ballades, and the sonatas.

Example for analysis, No. 13. Nocturne in F sharp minor, opus 48, No. 2.

The poise, variety, and nobility of the melodic line is the main thing to notice in the Nocturne, opus 48, No. 2. After two measures of introduction the central idea is announced in an aspiring two-measure phrase, immediately repeated in slightly elaborated form. Two more phrases of the same length, sequential and most imaginatively harmonized, lead to a repetition of the main idea, now in the dominant key of C sharp minor. The sequence recurs, but now in much expanded form as the accumulated emotion extends its second phrase to six measures. Observe the dignity of the stately movement in measures 20-22. A brief codetta on the theme brings a cadence, not in G sharp minor as we expect, but in the major. The whole is then repeated in slightly modified form.

The middle part, Molto più lento, D flat major, 3-4 time, on a most virile theme, contains interesting and powerful sequences and other harmonic devices. The imagination shown in the last twelve measures of it should be noticed, especially the ingenious return to the key of the first part.

This is now modified so as to end with a very lovely coda, quiet and at the same time noble.

CHAPTER VIII

Edvard Grieg

I

Nationalism in Music.

HE intense spirit of nationalism which swept over the people of Europe in the late sixties and the early seventies was felt and echoed in their work by many of the young musicians of the generation just then reaching maturity. Moussorgsky and Rimsky-Korsakoff in Russia, Smetana and Dvořák in Bohemia, and Grieg in Norway were leaders in the movement. Of them all, none is more popular than Grieg, whose piano pieces, not too difficult for the amateur and fascinating in their elusive charm, are played all over the world. Educated as a cosmopolitan musician, his choice of the idiom of his native land was the result not only of his temperamental bias, but of a deliberate determination to bring before the world the peculiar contribution to musical art which Norway had to offer.

Before his day, the music of the educated Norwegian was the music of Germany, of France, or Italy; the folk-tunes of Norway, with their modal and harmonic characteristics, were considered unworthy the attention of a serious artist. Grieg may be said to have added the musical dialect of his native country to the musical language of the world.

Early years.

Edvard Grieg, the son of Consul Alexander Grieg and his wife Gesine Hagerup Grieg, was born in Bergen, Norway, June 15, 1843. His father was of Scotch extraction, descended from a follower of the pretender, Charles Edward Stuart, who fleeing his country after the battle of Culloden, settled in Norway as a tradesman, and changing the spelling of his name from Greig to Grieg, in conformity to the Norwegian pronunciation, became thoroughly identified with his adopted country. His mother was of pure Norwegian blood, and of a family which had already given several famous men to the country. She was a woman of strong character and of decided artistic gifts. A well-educated musician, and recognizing the extraordinary endowment of her son, she became his first teacher and gave him, while yet a child, a thorough grounding in his art. It is said that at the age of nine he was so engrossed in music that, being asked by his school teacher to bring him a "composition," he wrote out some variations on a German melody, and presented them to the astonished master.

His artistic temperament showed itself in his keen appreciation of the beauties of the sombre northern landscape as well as in his love for music. At the age of fifteen he was still undecided whether he wished to become a painter or a musician, and it was the advice of Ole Bull, the celebrated violinist, which decided him and persuaded his parents to send him to Germany to study. He entered the Leipsic Conservatory in 1858, and with the exception of a few months spent at home recuperating from an attack of pulmonary trouble, a forerunner of the illness which harassed all his later life, he remained there continuously for four years, studying harmony, counterpoint and composition under Richter, Rietz and Reinecke, and piano under Wenzel and Moscheles.

Meeting with Nordraak.

It was in 1863, shortly after his graduation, that Grieg met Richard Nordraak, to whom he has paid eloquent tribute in his funeral march in A minor. In this gifted young man, doomed to an early death, he found a congenial friend whose magnetic personality and fervent patriotism made an undying impression upon him.

Together they studied the Norwegian folk-songs, and taking a solemn oath of musical allegiance, bound themselves to devote their lives to making from these crude beginnings a finished national art. "It was as though the scales fell from my eyes," writes Grieg. "For the first time I learned to understand my own nature. We abjured the Gade-Mendelssohn insipid and diluted Scandinavianism, and bound ourselves with enthusiasm to the new path which the Northern School is now following."

In 1864, together with their Danish friends Horneman and Matthison-Hansen, they formed the Euterpe Musical Society, for the performance of Scandinavian works, an institution which must have been an incalculable benefit and stimulus to their composition. Unfortunately, this happy association of young

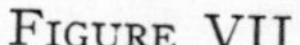

FIGURE VII

CHAP. VIII

artists was broken up by Nordraak's death, in 1866. The same year Grieg returned to Norway and settled in Christiania.

II

Norwegian Folk Music.

Like many other unsophisticated peoples, the Norwegians use certain melodic intervals derived rather from the ancient modes than from our modern major and minor scales, which gives their music a peculiar quaintness.

FIGURE VIII

From SLÄTTER, opus 72.

Shepherd's Boy, opus 54, No. 1.

Especially odd in its effect, because it interferes with the commonest of chord sequences, the dominant-tonic cadence with which most

pieces end, is the lowering of the "leading note," or seventh step of the scale, so called because of its strong tendency to lead up to the eighth (final) step. The phrases from Grieg's "Melodie," opus 47, No. 3, and "Berceuse," opus 38, No. 1, in Figure VII, show this flattened seventh step of the folk-music. The raised fourth step, also found in Norwegian as well as in Hungarian tunes, is well illustrated in his "Slätter," opus 72, and in "The Sheperd's Boy," opus 54, No. 1, and other of the Lyric Pieces. (See Figure VIII.)

When the leading tone is flattened it no longer pulls upward so powerfully, and may even fall to the fifth step of the scale; and it is notable that this peculiar melodic step is intensely characteristic both of Norwegian folk-song and of Grieg. The opening of his Piano Concerto is a striking instance of it. It will also be remarked between the fourth and fifth measures of the "Melodie" quoted in Figure 1, at the end of the phrase from the "Berceuse," and indeed on almost every page Grieg has written.

Peasant rhythms.

In rhythm as well as in melody, Grieg owes many of his most individual effects to Norwegian inspiration. Those bare open fifths in the bass with which so many of his pieces start out—the first Springtanz in the Northern Dances, for example—suggest the peasant bagpipe in an orgy of rhythm. Of the two best known national dances the Springtanz, named from the wild jumps or springs executed by the dancers, is in three-beat time, and in spite

Chap. VIII

of its energy is not devoid of grace; the Halling, in two-beat time,is march-like, and ,if anything, even more vigorous. On this latter type are based the four brilliantly developed "Norwegian Dances" of Grieg's opus 35. Several delicate rhythmic details that mark the composer's style are also traceable to the national source, such as the fondness for mingling the two-part and the three-part division of the beat in the same phrase, even in the same measure, and the so-called "weak cadence," in which the final chord comes on an unaccented beat.

III

Life in Christiania.

Shortly after his return to Norway, Grieg met and married his cousin, Miss Nina Hagerup, herself a musician and a delightful singer. Acting on the results of his experience in Copenhagen, Grieg founded in Christiania in 1867, a Musical Union for the promotion of Scandinavian music, and remained the conductor of the orchestra for the next seven years.

It was during these years, from the time he was twenty until his early thirties, that his most characteristic works were composed: the two Sonatas for Violin and Piano, opus 8 and 13; the Piano Sonata, opus 7; the incidental music to Ibsen's "Peer Gynt;" some of the most charming of the Lyric Pieces for piano and of the songs, and the Piano Concerto, opus 16:—the best part, certainly, of his entire musical output. Of all these, none are more delightful than his lovely and little-known songs, written under the inspiration of his artist wife's sympathetic co-operation, and interpreted by her with a singularly individual and intelligent beauty in their occasional joint concert appearances.

In 1865 and again in 1870, Grieg visited Italy, seeing much of Liszt in Rome. In 1879 he gave his brilliant piano concerto at Leipsic with great success. Aside from these journeyings his life in Christiania continued its even tenor, his time being devoted to composing or promoting the interests of music by teaching, concert work or musical reunions with fellow musicians. It is in these years that he seems to have reached the acme of his powers.

Individual qualities.

Grieg's music has, to a peculiar degree, that subtle quality we call personal flavor. Whatever the source of his melodies, whether they are taken from Norwegian tunes or invented fresh, he knows how to give them a setting which is entirely his own. As individuality is a trait indispensable to all art of real value, it is interesting to ask ourselves what are its hallmarks in any particular case. In Grieg's the most constant one is doubtless his harmonic subtlety and charm; his harmonic style is unlike any one else's; and in especial, he uses the chromatic scale as a basis for harmony with inimitable grace. In almost everything he has written one can find this scale somewhere, either in the middle voices or the bass, and in the majority of cases *descending.* The theme of the Ballade, opus 24, is a striking example. It is a tune that in itself suggests no special subtlety of harmony; it could readily be harmonized with the commonest chords of G minor and B flat major; yet, if after so harmonizing it, the student will compare Grieg's treatment, with its bass ever insidiously slipping away, he will understand the composer's art more deeply.

"Wall-paper patterns."

A less happy but equally persistent peculiarity is the breaking up of the music into very brief phrases, and the immediate repetition of them in new keys—the so-called "wall-paper patterns" of his mode of composition. This method of treatment may be partly traceable to the folk-songs, but it is even more due to a certain weakness of mental grasp, of logical coherence, characteristic of Grieg's mind. It has been the subject of severe criticism by those who demand above all of a composer the power to "compose"—to construct, organize, unfold. Thus M. Vincent d'Indy, in his "Cours de Composition Musicale,"* asserts that "the musical merit of Grieg is like that of a good miniature painter. His little works, whose melodic lines, often elegant and agreeable, exhaust themselves as if out of breath after a few charming measures, do not raise themselves very high. His short inspiration and his absolute ignorance of composition make him inapt in the construction of a symphonic work of any extent; he produces then only hybrid assemblages of short fragments, unskilfully sewed together or only juxtaposed, without any appearance of order or of unity

*Book II, Part I, page 419.

in conception and realization." Severe as this is, it must be admitted that it is supported by the analysis of the Violoncello Sonata that M. d'Indy proceeds to make. Grieg is indeed at his best in his miniatures—in such charming mood-pictures as the Lyric Pieces, the Album Leaves and the Songs.

Example for Analysis, No. 14. *Norwegian Dance, opus* 35, *No.* 1.

In the first of the "Norwegian Dances," a Halling tune, in D minor, Allegro marcato, is devéloped in various ways, sometimes in one hand and sometimes in the other. Note the characteristic chromatic harmonization, and the descent from seventh step to fifth in the left hand version of the melody. The climax ends in the "augmentation" of the sixteenth notes to eighth-notes.

The trio or contrast, in D major, Cantabile, is a bit of quiet and very lovely Grieg-like harmony. The chromatic scale will here and there be noticed. An ingenious touch is the preservation of the identical melody in the second half, while the key changes from D major to F sharp minor. Mr. Henry T. Finck, whose Grieg enthusiasm knows no bounds, says of this passage: "Only a genius could have written these ravishingly beautiful harmonies—a page which alone would suffice to make its author immortal."

Example for analysis, No. 15. *Allegro moderato from the Piano Sonata, opus* 7.

Grieg's Piano Sonata is a piece full of the early freshness and youthful energy of its composer, yet showing all too clearly the limitations which he never succeeded in transcending. As a *pot-pourri* of attractive melodies it is delightful; as a sonata it is a failure.

CHAP. VIII

The first theme, in E minor, discloses at once two motives which afterward dominate the development, the first a descending bit of "chord melody" in the first two measures, the second, in the following pair of measures, a scale melody, also descending and in a characteristic rhythm. Let us call them (a) and (b). With the thirteenth measure begins a rather pretentious canonic treatment of the theme, suggesting important contrapuntal evolutions, but quickly "petering out" into sonorous but musically empty passage work. The second theme, which commences in G major, near the middle of the second page, presents both the cadence 7-5 and the wall-paper pattern type of construction we associate with its composer. It is an attractive melody, but after four measures it seems to have exhausted the impulse which stirred it to life, and thereafter it can only rather helplessly repeat itself.

The development begins in E major, fortissimo, with the first theme. With the change to 6-8 time, however, motive (a) is abandoned and (b) in the bass provides the text of an interesting and original treatment until the recapitulation of the themes (marked "a tempo"). The second theme comes this time in E minor, and there is a short but stirring coda in which the chromatic scale comes strongly to the front.

IV

Later Life.

In 1874, when on receiving a government pension Grieg was enabled to resign the conductorship of the Musical Union and devote himself entirely to composition, the freshness of his invention had already begun to wane, and the spontaneity of his utterance to crystalize into mannerisms. It was but a few years later that Frederick Niecks wrote: "My fear in the case of Grieg always was that his love of Norwegian idioms would tend to narrow, materialize, and make shallow his conceptions, and prevent him from forming a style by imposing on him a manner." This seems to have been exactly what happened, with the result that he never acquired a mastery of the larger forms in music, and having done all that was possible to illuminate with his delightful genius the simple folk-tunes of his country, he spent his later years over-elaborating, transcribing, or paraphrasing the works of his youth.

He traveled on the continent and in England in 1888 and 1889, giving concerts of his works and song-recitals with his wife. In 1894 he again visited England, and received the degree of Musical Doctor from Cambridge University. The rest of his life was spent at his picturesque villa, Troldhangen, a few miles from Bergen, where he died, September 4, 1907.

Personal appearance.

In Tschaikowsky's "Diary of My Tour in 1888" we get a vivid description of Grieg as he appeared in middle life. Tschaikowsky writes: "During the rehearsal of Brahms's new trio, as I was taking the liberty of making some remarks as to the skill and execution of

Chap. VIII

the relative tempo 2-3—remarks which were very good-naturedly received by the composer —there entered the room a very short, middle-aged man, exceedingly fragile in appearance, with shoulders of unequal height, fair hair brushed back from his forehead, and a very slight, almost boyish beard and mustache. There was nothing very striking about the features of this man, whose exterior at once attracted my sympathy, for it would be impossible to call them handsome or regular; but he had an uncommon charm, and blue eyes, not very large, but irresistibly fascinating, recalling the glance of a charming and candid child. I rejoiced in the depths of my heart when we were introduced to each other, and it turned out that this personality, which was so inexplicably sympathetic to me, belonged to a musician whose warmly emotional music had long ago won my heart. He proved to be the Norwegian composer Edvard Grieg."

Grieg in Paris.

A year later, the French critic Ernest Closson described Grieg, who was then playing and conducting his works in Paris, in these terms: "Grieg is small, thin, and narrow-shouldered. His body, which is like a child's, is always in motion—the movements short, lively, singularly jerky and angular, each step shaking the whole body and hitching the shoulders as if he limped; a 'bundle of nerves', to use a doctor's phrase of picturesque energy. The head, which looks massive on so small a body, is intelligent and very handsome, with long grayish hair thrown back, thin face, smoothly shaven chin, short, thick mustache, small but full nose, and eyes!—eyes superb, green, gray, in which one can fancy one catches a glimpse of Norway, with its melancholy fjords and its luminous mists. His gaze is serious, wonderfully soft, with a peculiar expression, at once worn, tentative, and childishly naïve. The entire effect is of kindness, candor, a sincere modesty."

Summary.

These descriptions of the man as he appeared to his contemporaries give us a vivid impression of his personality as well as of his physical appearance. He was evidently of a singularly nervous, sensitive temperament, keenly alive to delicate shades of beauty. His artistic expression has just these qualities, and is of value most of all because it is the expression of delicate personal feeling. It is subjective, intimate, and intangible, of delightful finesse and charming whimsicality.

With the virtues of this lyric expression he has its shortcomings. The structure of his work is always simple, the phrases short, as in the folk-tunes on which he modeled it. His harmonic methods and melodic and rhythmic peculiarities are so persistent as to become mannerisms. But with all the limitations which his lyricism imposes, the fact remains that Grieg has added a volume of rare charm and beauty to the musical literature of the world.

CHAPTER IX

Antonin Dvorák

I

Contrast between Grieg and Dvorák.

TWO years before the birth of Grieg in Norway, Antonin Dvořák, a composer destined to accomplish for Bohemian music what Grieg did for Scandinavian folk-song, was born in a small village of Bohemia. Although their lives covered nearly an identical span of years and their services to their art had much in common, their circumstances, their characters, and their types of genius were in sharp contrast. Grieg's youth was passed in surroundings most favorable to the growth of his talent: his mother was a cultivated musician, his father was a man of education and standing in the community. Dvořák was the son of the village innkeeper and butcher; the family means were restricted and the environment of the simplest. Grieg was of a gentle, fastidious and charming disposition; Dvořák was simple and undiscriminating, persistent with the dogged persistence of his peasant ancestry. Grieg, cultivated in the study of cosmopolitan

Chap. IX

music, deliberately restricted himself to the exploitation of the folk-music of his native land. Dvořák, springing from the soil, and passing his youth among the peasant singers and players, only later learned of the music beyond the confines of his country and of cosmopolitan art. So, although the two composers were contemporaneous, and although they were both workers in the idioms of their native lands, they approached music from opposite poles, and may be said to have met on common ground only in passing. Grieg came from the study of music in general to the study of the music of his country, and stopped there; Dvořák, beginning with the peasant tunes which his mother sang at his cradle, reached out into the wider world of music in his maturity. Grieg, going from the general to the particular, reached the zenith of his attainment in his early manhood; Dvořák, ever seeking broader fields, was at the height of his powers in his later years.

Early life.

Dvořák was born September 8, 1841, at Mühlhausen (Nelahozeves), in Bohemia, the eldest son in a family of eight children. As soon as he was of proper age he was sent with the children of the neighborhood to the little village school to learn to read and write. But, although his father was a man of simple tastes and small means, he was evidently not without ambition for his family, and finding that his son was worthy of a more complete education than could be had in Mühlhausen he sent him, in 1853, to live with his uncle in

CHAP. IX

Zolnitz and attend the school there. It was in Zolnitz that Dvořák began to study music, taking lessons in organ, piano playing, and theory. Two years later he went to a school in Kamnitz that he might learn German, and here he continued his music lessons under another master.

A sad fiasco.

His general education finished, he returned home hoping to persuade his father to let him go into music as a profession. By way of giving convincing proof of his ability, he composed, as a surprise for some family festival, a polka to be played by the village band. Unfortunately, he who was destined to become pre-eminent as an orchestral writer had not yet learned to write for the trumpet, a transposing instrument. The result was that, as he had written the trumpet parts where they were to be sounded rather than where they should be played to produce the required tones, the discords surpassed the composer's power of explanation, and his father was more loath than ever to see what promised to be a good butcher spoiled for a bad musician. Dvořák's native persistence came to his aid, however, and he eventually got permission to go to Prague to study under Pitzsch at the Organ School.

Years of study in Prague.

For the first few months his father was able to send him a modest allowance for his support; but soon that ceased, and Dvořák found himself dependent entirely on his own exertions. Nowhere in the history of music do we read a story of greater privation than that which young Dvořák endured for the next few years. Playing the viola in cafés to earn a few pennies a day, living on the scantiest and cheapest food, and in every way economizing his hard-earned money and his time that he might continue his music lessons, he persisted with a dogged, unthinking perseverance in the path he had chosen for himself.

In spite of the moral which one might try to draw from Dvořák's career of the blessing of poverty, the only possible advantage which this early privation gave him was that which he got from the enforced intimacy with the players of the band. From them he learned all the tricks of the trade, all the shades and gradations in the differing registers of the instruments, all the subtle variations in the production of tone, and the countless details which merged with his native genius to make him the wonderful necromancer of the orchestra which he became in later years. Playing in the streets in the day time and in the cafés by night, Dvořák was able to scrape together about nine dollars a month, and on this frugal income he managed to survive. It was seldom he could hear any good music. We read of a performance of the opera "Der Freischütz," which he would fain have heard could he have gathered together the four pennies necessary to pay his admittance, and we learn of various orchestral masterpieces which he was able to overhear only from his hiding place in the shadow of the friendly kettledrums, but of score reading there was none,

Chap. IX

as he could not afford to buy scores, nor were they available in the libraries.

II

Early compositions.

After his graduation from the Organ School, in 1860, his circumstances gradually improved. Smetana, who stood at the head of the Bohemian school of composers, became interested in him, lent him scores of the classic symphonies and chamber works, and got him a position in the orchestra of the National Theatre. Karel Bendl, conductor of the choral society, helped him in his studies and was in every way a kind friend to him. For the next ten years Dvorák studied and composed in seclusion, laying the foundation of his later success. It was not until 1873, when he was appointed organist of St. Adelbert's church on a salary which enabled him to give up his position in the theatre orchestra and organize on his own initiative a private class in music, that he began to receive the fruits of his strenuous apprenticeship.

Marriage.

In the same year he married, and under the protection of a tranquil and happy domestic life began to pour forth the flood of compositions which he continued uninterruptedly for the rest of his life. The first work which to any degree aroused the interest of the public was the cantata "The Heirs of the White Mountains," written in 1873.

A persistent will.

Shortly after this success there followed one of the most peculiar and characteristic episodes of Dvořák's career. He received a commission from the National Theatre, founded especially for the furtherance of Bohemian art, to write an opera. Then, if ever, one would think, was the opportunity for him to use the stores of folk-music with which his mind was saturated. But it chanced that at the moment Dvořák was under the spell of Wagner, and with his usual oblivion of everything but what was of musical interest to him at the time he must needs write for this theatre devoted to Bohemian art, music in imitation of the latest German expression. The result was that the audience was mystified and bored and the opera made a flat failure. Realizing his mistake, he painstakingly set to work and rewrote the entire score. This time it was not the music, but the libretto, which failed to please; so the libretto was rewritten, and with nothing of the original work left but the title, "The King and the Collier," the opera made its third and wholly successful appearance. The next year the revised version was given in Vienna, and won for the composer a government pension of two hundred and fifty dollars, an amount which was later increased.

Foreign appreciation.

An acquaintance with Brahms, which proved of great value to Dvořák, came about when the German composer was acting as judge in a competition to which Dvořák had submitted several works, including the delightful collection of duets "Klänge aus Mähren." As a result of the ensuing friendship between the musicians Dvořák met the publisher Simrock and was commissioned by him to write a series of Slavonic dances, which met with instantaneous favor from the public. Dvořák was now fairly launched. Joachim introduced his works into England and Germany: the dances were played at the Crystal Palace in 1879, and shortly after his Stabat Mater, sung first in London by the London Musical Society (an amateur association) in 1876, was given in public with enormous success. In 1884 Dvořák visited England and conducted the work at Albert Hall, and the following autumn at the Worcester Festival. A year later he was engaged to write a cantata ("The Spectral Bride") for the Birmingham Festival, which was produced with success. In 1889 he was decorated by the Austrian Court, and in 1890 he received the degree of Doctor of Music at Cambridge.

An early riser.

It was of the visit to England which Dvořák made to receive this degree that Sir Charles Villiers Stanford writes in his memoirs, giving us a quaint picture of the musician and his wife rising in the early morning, long before the household was aroused, and sitting in the dewy garden beneath their host's bedroom windows, patiently awaiting the sophisticated breakfast hour.

III

National elements in Dvořák's style.

The mercurial temperament of the Bohemians shows itself in the extreme contrasts of mood of their native music. It varies from wild hilarity to heart-broken sadness, often in the same short piece, and with transitions so sudden as almost to take away one's breath. Perhaps on the whole the more joyous mood is the more characteristic of this buoyantly healthy race. There is an inexhaustible freshness of vital energy in their dances, such as the polka and the furiant, introduced into chamber music by Smetana and Dvořák, and the prevailing tone of their artistic music, as of the folk music, is undoubtedly a sort of innocent and happy naivete. This works itself out in a peculiar and very characteristic irresponsibility of high spirits. In rhythm, for example, there is an immense energy that animates not only the chief melody, but all the subordinate parts. Everything bubbles in a score of Dvořák's, as everything doubtless bubbled in the bands in which he used to play as a penniless boy in Prague. He reflects also the eccentric rhythms of three and five measures in which his countrymen delight, as if they were almost consciously playing truant from the schools of German regularity.

Chromatic harmony.

Even more strikingly does this spirit of impulsive spontaneity affect their harmonies and modulations. As Mr. Hadow has pointed out in his admirable essay on Dvořák.* Bohemia was left untouched by the diatonic scale system that dominated most European countries, and as a result "To Dvořák the chromatic passages are part of the essential texture, and the most extreme modulations follow as simply and easily as the most obvi-

*"Studies in Modern Music," by W. H. Hadow, Second Series.

ous." The student may well ponder the eight measures from the "Klänge aus Mähren" shown in Figure IX. The rhythm in this case is monotonous—exactly the same in each one of the eight; but the ingenuity and unexpectedness of the modulation is such that our ears are kept constantly on the *qui vive*. As the

Figure IX

From the "Klänge aus Mähren."

present writer has elsewhere pointed out: "Dvořák loves to descend unexpectedly upon the most remote keys, never knows where he will turn next, and when he gets too far from home returns over fences and through no-thoroughfares." This richness of tonal background adds a truly exotic quality to those movements based on the more melancholy phase of the national temper, especially the beautiful "Dumkas" (Elegies) which he has incorporated in his A Major Piano Quintet, in his third symphony, and in his six elegies for piano trio.

Example for analysis, No. 16. Slavonic Dance, opus 46, No. 1.

Stainer remarks in his "Composition" that "subdivisions of the strong pulse are very frequently met with in movements of a playful character." The division of the first beat so persistent in this spirited folk-theme undoubtedly gives it some of its pronounced animation; and this effect is enhanced by the strong cross accents, on the third and fifth beats of the two-measure phrase, with complete omission of stress on the fourth, where the regular metrical stress should fall. Here, then, is a finely vigorous specimen of folk-rhythm. In modulatory initiative the dance is also "true to type." Scarcely does it begin to develop before it whips off into A major; a little later it passes through the original key of C over into G, first major and then minor; and so it comes naturally to F, the subdominant of the home key, where the main theme is vigorously reaffirmed. The soft codetta, with its persistent echoings of bits of the

CHAP. IX

theme, illustrates what was said of the bubbling life of the subordinate parts in Dvořák.

The Trio is in A major. Here, after sixteen measures of new theme have been given out, development is immediately begun with the theme in the bass, and a new effervescence of accompanying melody above it, all modulating freely. Note the charming addition, at the pianissimo return of the theme in a middle voice, of a quicker version of it above, which later, by "double counterpoint," changes places with it. A gradual climax then leads back to the main subject. At the end is a brief coda in which the salient rhythmic figure of this (the opening three notes) is combined with the melody of the Trio.

IV

Stay in New York.

In 1892 Dvořák was induced to come to the United States as Director of the National Conservatory of Music in New York. He was welcomed by a grand concert given in his honor, was cordially received by the musicians of the country, and was the recipient of a salary which might well have seemed fabulous to him five or ten years earlier. During his stay of three years in this country he became much interested in the negro music of the Southern States, which seemed to him to fill the place of folk-music in America. Putting his belief into practice, he wrote a symphony ("From the New World"), a quartet, and a quintet, based on negro themes, which rank among the finest of his works. The slow movement of the symphony, especially, tinged perhaps by the homesickness which never quite left him in this alien atmosphere, is of a poignant beauty which he never surpassed.

In 1895 Dvořák decided rather suddenly to give up his American position, and returned to Prague. Six years later he was appointed to the directorship of the Prague Conservatory, a post which he continued to hold until his death in May, 1904.

Influence of negro music.

Dvořák has by no means slavishly copied the slaves' music in his three so-called "American" works. There are no literal transcriptions of tunes. The second theme of the allegro of the "New World Symphony" recalls "Swing Low, Sweet Chariot"; the scherzo of the quintet has a touch of "Old Man Moses, He Sells Roses"; but beyond that there are few striking resemblances of detail, and indeed even the general atmosphere is as much Bohemian as it is negro. The scherzos of the third and of the fifth symphonies sound as much alike as if their composer had not made his acquaintance with America between the dates of their composition. One may be labelled "Czech" and the other "Negro"; both *sound* unmistakably "Dvořák."

Yet there are some of the negro peculiarities in these compositions. A number of the themes, for instance, are founded on the pentatonic scale (of five notes), so much used by negroes*. The theme of the first movement of the quartet is an example; the theme of the first movement of the symphony uses the minor form of this scale; the beautiful melody of the famous Largo in the same symphony approximates it closely.

The peculiar melancholy of negro music is due in no small measure to a cadence constantly found in it—a cadence which for the dominant-tonic chords of our ordinary cadence substitutes the succession of a major triad and its relative minor, as, for example, C-E-G followed by A-C-E-A. The effect is often enhanced by an uncertain indecisive see-sawing back and forth from one to the other. In a moment we shall see how appealingly Dvořák employs this cadence.

But, after all, the outstanding feature of the negro song and its musical cousins is, of course, that curious rhythmic jerk, that jump away from the normally accented note to another longer one which usurps its stress, which we call "rag-time." This is found both in merry and in sad tunes, and applied with great ingenuity and resourcefulness. It is not peculiar, by the way, to negro music, being found in the so-called "Scotch snap," in Hungarian folk-tunes, and elsewhere; but by no people has it been used with such nervous energy and such whimsical piquancy of effect as by our dark-skinned musicians. The student will find

*This is the scale obtained by playing the black keys of the piano, beginning with F♯. In it the fourth and seventh steps of the ordinary scale are wanting.

it on many pages of the Dvořák pieces, as, for instance, in the main themes of the quartet and the symphony first movements.

Example for analysis, No. 17. Largo from the "New World Symphony."

After some mysterious chromatic harmonies in the brass and low wood-wind instruments, and a few quiet chords on the muted strings, the English horn sings its hauntingly beautiful melody, full of a childlike wistfulness. It is slightly developed in the strings after a return of the opening passage for high wood-wind. At its end, muted horns once more suggest its opening figure, but pause, as if hesitant, on a single A flat.

A contrasting theme now enters, on flute and oboe, with the change of signature to four sharps, over a mere breath of accompaniment in tremolo strings. It is in this theme that the student will find the touching major-minor cadences of the negro music mentioned above. A more deliberately soaring melody, also in C-sharp minor, alternates with it, over a persistent and strangely expressive bass plucked by the low strings. After this has twice recurred, there is a charming change of mode from minor to major, and with this brightening, as of the reappearing sun on a cloudy day, one instrument after another (oboe, clarinet, flute, violins, basses) plays a dancing little pastoral theme in staccato sixteenth notes. As this climaxes we hear an emphatic announcement of the main theme from the first movement, soon dying away again to an impressive quiet in which the main

English horn melody again breathes forth. This time it is interrupted by impressive pauses, as if it lost courage to continue; the mysterious chromatic chords are heard for one last time from solemn, soft trombones, and with two organ-like chords from double basses alone this wonderful movement dies into silence.

Summary.

The mere volume of Dvořák's work is extraordinary. He poured out music with an ease and facility in which he rivals Schubert, that bubbling spring of music. He wrote cantatas, oratorios and hymns for chorus and orchestra, a mass, a requiem, and nine operas, five symphonies, five overtures, symphonic poems and various other orchestral pieces, concertos for piano, violin and violoncello, quintets, quartets and trios for strings, and all sorts of combinations for chamber music, besides piano pieces and songs. In all his music his extraordinarily felicitous melody, his vital rhythms, his rich color-schemes make an irresistible appeal. In his orchestration he ranks with Berlioz and Wagner as a supreme master. In his simple spontaneous melodies he may well compare with Schubert, and in the elasticity of his rhythms and his fascinating and arbitrary treatment of tonality he is unique, and charms with a freshness and felicity that is child-like in its effect of unpremeditated waywardness. Indeed, there is something child-like both in the man himself and in his work, and we shall lose much of the value of his service to his art if we persist in demanding of him the thoughtful expressions which only a man of an entirely different temperament could have given us, and do not take him simply for what he was—a musician with a marvelous instinct for charming combinations of tone and tonal color.

CHAPTER X

CAMILLE SAINT-SAËNS

I

A modern classicist.

N an article on "Anarchy in Music," Saint-Saëns, a keen critic of the art he practices so skilfully, has made vivid by a striking antithesis the classicism of taste that distinguishes him from most of his contemporaries. According to the ultra-modernists, he says, "He whose musical sensibility is properly developed is not he who, tasting wine, can give you the growth and the vintage year. It is he who partakes with equal tolerance of heavy wine or light, whiskey or brandy, preferring that which most burns his throat. It is not he who in judging a picture appreciates the delicate touches by means of which the different tones blend with each other, but he who brutally brings together vermilion and Verona green, as one sees at the exhibition in Autumn. It is not he who, in music, appreciates ingeniously contrived changes of tonality, giving the theme new and undreamt-of significance, as the great Richard does all through the score of "Die Meister-

Chap. X.

singer"; it is he who, being at home in all the tonalities, unceasingly piles up dissonances never prepared and never resolved, snorting his way through the musical field like a wild boar in a flower garden." The hatred of crudity, the love of delicate discriminations and accurate adjustments, shown in this criticism, have throughout his long career been characteristic of the most typical of modern French composers, the man who, in spite of some aridity of temperament, has won a permanent place in music by the exercise of those most gallic of traits, lucidity, sense of proportion, sense of style, *esprit*.

II

Early years.

Camille Saint-Saëns, born in Paris in 1835, began the study of the piano at the age of three, composed little waltzes at five, and at ten could play fugues of Bach and concertos by Hummel, Mozart, and Beethoven. In 1846 the *Gazette Musicale* of Paris announced a concert in the Salle Pleyel at which "Le petit Saint-Saëns" played a concerto of Mozart, "without notes, with no effort, giving his phrases with clearness, elegance, and even expression in the midst of the powerful effects of a numerous orchestra using all its resources." It is interesting to add that the same composer played the same concerto in the same hall exactly fifty years later at the golden jubilee of his artistic début, held in Paris in 1896. Saint-Saëns entered the Paris Conservatoire at the age of twelve, studied

CHAP. X.

composition with Benoist and Halévy, and produced a symphony at sixteen.

A typical Frenchman.

The wit and finesse of all he did, so typically French, won him an enviable position in Parisian artistic and social circles from the first. We read how, at Mme. Garcia's house, he would pass from improvising "masterly pages" in the contrapuntal style to waltzes for the young people's dancing. He had also for many years a sort of salon of his own—his famous Mondays. One of his habitual guests thus describes him as he was in those days: "Saint-Saëns is of short stature. His head is extremely original, the features characteristic: a great brow, wide and open, where, between the eyebrows, the energy and the tenacity of the man reveal themselves; hair habitually cut short, and brownish beard turning gray; a nose like an eagle's beak, underlined by two deeply marked wrinkles starting from the nostrils; eyes a little prominent, very mobile, very expressive. The familiars of his Mondays . . . remember that there was about him a keen animation, a diabolic mischievousness, a railing irony, and an agility in leaping in talk from one subject to another . . . that equalled the mobility of his features."

And a voluminous writer.

An evidence more permanent than his talk of the insatiable intellectual curiosity of Saint-Saëns is to be found in his published prose writings, singularly voluminous for a man to whom criticism was after all only a relaxation in a creative life. Hardly more than half of them are directly concerned with music. The two volumes "Harmonie et Melodie" and "Portraits et Souvenirs" contain musical essays on a great variety of subjects. An interest in philosophy is revealed in the book on "Problèms et Mystères"; he becomes an archeologist in his "Note sur les décors de théâtre dans l'antiquité romaine; and in the "Rimes familières," and the comedy "La crampe des écrivains" he appears in the rôles of poet and of dramatist.

III

Saint-Saëns as a symphonist.

So versatile a mind as this would naturally confine itself to no one province of its chosen art, and Saint-Saëns has been equally successful in symphony, chamber-music, piano pieces, programme music, and opera. We may look first at his very characteristic contributions to pure music—music without words or programmes. Here the most important items are five concertos for piano, three for violin, one for violoncello; the "Trumpet Septet," an early quartet and quintet with piano, the well-known violoncello sonata, Opus 34, as well as sonatas for violin; a fine string quartet; and above all, the three symphonies, at the head of which stands the Symphony in C minor with piano and organ, Opus 78.

The intellectual element in his work.

Taken as a whole these works give a striking reflection of the essential character of their composer's mind, keenly intellectual, fond of clear outline and subtle development, somewhat deficient in primal emotion. All his musical ideas are, in the words of his contempo-

Chap. X.

rary and fellow-countryman, M. Vincent d'Indy, "a little dry and lacking in warm expansiveness" ("un peu sèches et dépourvues d'expansion chaleureuse").* For this reason, indeed, some critics have denied him the qualification "classic," and substituted "pseudo-classic." Seldom do we find in his works a melody of broad sweep, of passionate expressiveness. He prefers, as Beethoven before him preferred, to take a brief phrase, a fragment of a few notes, and build out of it gradually, by ingenious rhythmic and other modifications, a complete structure. The vast C minor Symphony, for instance, his masterpiece in pure music, is like an oak of which four notes form the acorn—the four notes shown in a few of their chief transformations in Figure X. Now this eminently intellectual mode

Figure X

*V. d'Indy: Cours de Composition Musicale. IIme Livre, Ire Partie, p. 427.

of composition is entirely successful only when it is fructified by emotion, and most of his critics agree that it is not always so fructified in Saint-Saëns. "Certain of his works," says M. Georges Servières,* "seem as empty as others are ingenious. The workmanship is always remarkable; it is the fundamental ideas that sometimes fail to impress us with their originality." And M. d'Indy concludes his estimate by saying: "Whatever the value of his ideas, it is always enhanced by a most interesting treatment, for which at least he deserves to be classed in the first rank of the artists of our time."

His rhythmic vigor.

Saint-Saëns has himself pointed out, however, in his "Harmonie et Melodie," that the importance of melody may be exaggerated. He speaks of the "furious war against all serious music, the hypocritical enthusiasm for song and melody, deceitful labels of which I have tried to show the meaninglessness," and justly protests: "There are melodic ideas, and rhythmic ideas, and harmonic ideas. It is not only melodies that constitute ideas." His own ideas, in fact, are often harmonic or contrapuntal (for he is a devout student of Bach and one of the greatest modern masters of counterpoint, as the opening of his G minor Piano Concerto is alone enough to show), and still oftener rhythmic. It may safely be said that no modern composer save Brahms has excelled him in rhythmic interest and variety

*La Musique Française Moderne.

CHAP. X.

—the final test, perhaps, of the intellectual quality in music.

IV

Love of the picturesque.

The same intellectual curiosity that has prompted Saint-Saëns to investigate so deeply the world of tones and their combinations has carried him all over the physical world. He has been a tireless traveler. For many years he spent his winters in the Canary Islands, and there is probably no corner of earth that he has not visited, often incognito. In one of his essays he gives us the key to this taste for wandering—a love of the unusual, the outlandish, the picturesque. In describing the academic procession at the University of Cambridge in 1893, when he received a doctor's degree, he says: "At the head marched the King of Bahonagar, in a gold turban, sparkling with fabulous gems, a necklace of diamonds at his throat," and adds: "Dare I avow that, as an enemy of the banalities and the dull tones of our modern garments, I was enchanted with the adventure?"

And of adventure.

This love of adventure is reflected in such works as the "Nuit à Lisbonne," the "Jota Aragonese," and the "Rapsodie d'Auvergne," depicting scenes in Southern Europe, the Suite Algerienne with its vivid pictures of the Algerian desert, and the fantasy "Africa," Opus 89. The most famous of the works in this picturesque style, however, and justly so, are undoubtedly the four symphonic poems, "Phaéton," the "Danse Macabre," "La Jeunesse d'Hercule," and "Le Rouet d'Omphale." Here his method is in many respects the same as in the abstract works, but a new flavor is added by the use of the program.

Example for analysis, No. 18.

*"Le Rouet d'Omphale."**

The composer uses the perfectly free form known as the "symphonic poem," described in connection with the example from Liszt, "Les Preludes." In that work there were two themes, of almost equal importance. In "Le Rouet d'Omphale," on the other hand, there is only one main theme, sometimes called "Omphale's blandishment," which is heard in three rhythmically varied states, and with which is contrasted the subordinate theme of Hercules' struggles. The remainder of the material is derived from the ingenious figure suggesting the whir of the spinning-wheel.

The subject of this work, according to the composer himself, is "feminine seduction, the triumph of weakness over strength." "The spinning-wheel," he tells us, "is but a pretext, chosen solely with a view to the rhythm and the general effect of the piece."

It is perhaps not too fantastic to see in the opening passages a musical picture of the starting into motion of the spinning-wheel. That apparent condensing of the image which is often noticed when a wheel revolves more and more rapidly the composer suggests by beginning with a wide arpeggio figure, covering more than an octave span, and gradually reducing it to a trill. With the Allegro, 6-8,

*Omphale's Spinning-Wheel. Omphale was a Lydian princess and the mistress of Hercules.

Chap. X.

in A major, the motion becomes well established, and after eighteen preliminary measures the theme of Omphale's blandishment starts in softly, marked "graziosamente," in its first rhythmic variant, the notes of the melody coming on beats one, two, and four, five of each measure. The whirring goes on ceaselessly in the accompaniment. This theme is developed deliberately, and with many effective changes between loud and soft.

Before long we hear it a second time, but now most ingeniously transformed. Its rhythm is syncopated in such a way that the notes now come on beats two, three, and five, six, —in other words "against" the measure accents instead of with them. The student will note how piquant is this rhythm. The theme undergoes much interesting elaboration, both rhythmic and harmonic, before arriving at the high trill on B sharp and C sharp under which the secondary theme (of Hercules' "groaning under the bonds he cannot break," according to the composer) starts in heavily and as it were wearily in the bass ("pesante" C-sharp minor). This is one long and powerfully cumulative climax, at the end of which great poignancy of expression is attained by the strong dissonances and bold leaps of the melody. The passion dies down again, wearily, hopelessly, and in the soft Gs the utter dejection of the hero is depicted.

In the "Meno mosso" the composer tells us we may fancy we hear "Omphale laughing at the vain efforts of the hero." There is a curious descending phrase, four times repeated, that seems to suggest the teasing sympathy of the lady, and with the return of the Allegro she dismisses his troubles from her mind and returns to her spinning. This time (2-4, A major, tranquillo e scherzando) the main theme takes its final and most piquant rhythmic form—it is reduced to even eighth notes, two to each group of six in the accompaniment.

An amusing touch is reserved for the end, where the spinning-wheel gradually stops revolving. Everyone has noticed, in a wheel thus "running down," the tendency to stop at a certain point, the heaviest of all, beyond which it is carried nevertheless, again and again, but each time with greater difficulty, by its momentum. Is not this "sticking point" irresistibly suggested by the D sharps of the closing measures?

V

Summary.

Saint-Saëns has been indefatigably active in other fields besides those of chamber-music and the symphony, concerto, and symphonic poem. Curiously enough, although he was organist of the Madeleine from 1858 to 1877, he has written comparatively little for organ. But he has produced much choral music, both sacred and secular, at the head of which doubtless stands his well-known opera, "Samson et Dalila." He has also written a great many songs and piano pieces, the latter brilliant but of comparatively little musical inter-

Chap. X.

est. As the writer has elsewhere said,* music at the present day has a real need for artists of Saint-Saëns' type. "Their office is to make us remember, in our welter of emotion, the perennial delightfulness of order and control. They are the apologists of reason, without which feeling, however noble, must become futile, inarticulate. In their precise, well-constructed works we find a relief from the dissipating effects of mere passion. We breathe there a serene, if a somewhat rarefied atmosphere. Of this classic luciditv Saint-Saëns is a great master. However dry he may sometimes be, he is never turgid; however superficial his thought, it is never vague; he offers us his artistic sweets never in the form of syrup—he refines and crystallizes them. If, then, we find his music sometimes empty for all its skill, we must not for that reason underrate the service he does for music by insisting on articulateness in feeling, logic in development, and punctilious finesse in workmanship."

*From Grieg to Brahms.

CHAPTER XI

César Franck

I

Contrast between Franck and Saint-Saëns.

F we should search in all the literature of music we could find few greater contrasts in both form and content than we find between Saint-Saëns and his contemporary, César Franck. Both men were living out their active life in Paris at the same time, the musical atmosphere about them was the same, their training was alike, their musical inheritance the same; but the divergence in their characters, their temperaments, and their art was almost complete.

As we have seen, Saint-Saëns is a man of the world, of social aplomb, finesse, and address; César Franck was a simple, drudging teacher and artist, with no thought of fashionable life, and little consciousness of practical details. There is a like difference in their work: Saint-Saëns' music shows the vitality and intellectual clarity of his mind, Franck's reveals the mysticism, the spiritual intensity of

Chap. XI

his. The one is an artist by virtue of his intellect and power of fancy, the other by virtue of his emotional and imaginative strength.

Franck's descent and early life.

César Franck was born in Liège, Belgium, December 10, 1822. The Francks claim descent from a family of Walloon painters, one of whom, Jérome Franck (1540-1610), emigrated to Paris and became the court painter of Henry III. The tradition of artistry seems to have been handed down in the family. Although César Franck's father was himself in the banking business, he early decided that his sons should become professional musicians and educated them with that intention. It is not unusual to read of the triumph of supreme talent in spite of the opposition of practical parents, or, on the other hand, of mediocre talents fostered by doting relatives; but here is the exceptional case of a supposedly practical father insisting that his sons throw prudence to the winds and take up with the precarious career of the musician. Fortunately, as far as his son César was concerned, he could not have made a better choice had he been gifted with supernatural foresight. So well did the boy profit by his instruction, that at the age of twelve he had completed his studies at the music school in Liège, and the following year was entered as a pupil at the Paris Conservatoire, taking composition under Léborne and piano with Zimmermann.

A "Grand Prize" at the Paris Conservatory.

At the end of his first year's work at the Conservatoire he was awarded a *proxime accessit;* but in the competition for pianoforte in

1838, his very cleverness was nearly his undoing. M. Vincent d'Indy relates the incident in his book on "César Franck" in the following words:

"After having played the work selected—Hummel's A minor Concerto—in excellent style, young Franck took it into his head, when it came to the sight-reading test, to transpose the piece which was put before him to the third below, playing it off without the least slip or hesitation.

"Such exploits were not within the rules of the competition, and this audacity on the part of a pupil of fifteen and a half so shocked old Cherubini, then Director of the Conservatoire, that he stoutly declined to award a first prize to the lad, although he deserved it. But in spite of his redtapism and dictatorial methods, the composer of 'Lodoiska' was not really unjust, and proposed to the jury to recommend the audacious pianist for a special reward, outside all competition, and known by the high-sounding title of 'Grand Prix d'Honneur.' This is the only time, to my knowledge, that such a prize has been given at any instrumental competition in the Paris Conservatoire."

Skill in counterpoint.

In the next two years Franck won first prizes in fugue. In 1841, his surpassing ability, which enabled him to combine in improvisation the theme given for a fugue subject with that announced for a "free composition," again bewildered the judges so that they at first proposed to give him no recognition whatever, and were only persuaded by his teacher's explanation of his feat, to award him a second prize.

For some reason which has never been made public, at this point in his studies, when Franck was just beginning his work for the competition for the "Prix de Rome," his father suddenly withdrew him from the Conservatoire. It is evident that his father intended him to follow the career of a piano virtuoso, and his teachers gave him the same advice, but nothing was further from Franck's natural tastes. After two years spent in Belgium, where he did not receive the royal patronage which his father had manœuvred for and counted upon, the family moved back to Paris, and the two sons, assuming the household's support, accepted what teaching and concert playing they could get.

II

Early compositions.

It was during the years spent in the Conservatoire and the years immediately following that Franck wrote his early piano pieces. Although these are of comparatively little value, they contain certain innovations of interest especially to pianists. A few vocal pieces, the oratorio "Ruth," and four Trios also date from this period. Of the Trios, two were introduced to German audiences by Franz Liszt, who greeted the young composer with the generous interest he was so glad to bestow on struggling talent. The Trio in F minor is the only one of the four which gives us any foretaste of Franck's later work. In the others, as well as in the piano pieces and vocal works, Franck is still in the student period, showing too evidently the influence of Beethoven in the chamber music, of Liszt in the piano pieces, and of Mehul and the eighteenth century composers in the vocal works.

Marriage and new start in life.

Hardly was Franck settled in Paris, when his prospects, which had seemed so hopeful, darkened about him. The political situation became increasingly alarming, many people felt it discreet to leave town, and Franck lost most of his pupils. He had been affianced for some months to a young actress, Mlle. Desmousseaux, and now, despite the bad times and the disapproval of his parents, who saw themselves deprived of a substantial prop for their support, he decided to marry immediately. The wedding took place in the midst of the Revolution of 1848, the wedding party making their way through the barricaded streets to the church.

A methodical and obscure life.

With his marriage began the methodical life of drudgery which Franck supported with unfailing cheerfulness, almost with enthusiasm, as long as he lived. Setting aside two hours of the early morning for what he called his "own work"—reading, study, or composition—the rest of the day was given to teaching or practice. His pupils lived all over Paris. From morning till night he went from lesson to lesson, so eager to be at work that he ran rather than walked along the streets.

Organist at Sainte Clotilde.

In 1858 Franck was appointed organist of Sainte Clotilde, and here, "in the dust of this organ loft," as M. Vincent d'Indy says in his biography, "he spent the best part of his life. Here he came every Sunday and feast-day—and toward the end of his life every Friday morning too—fanning the fire of his genius by pouring out his spirit in wonderful improvisations which were often far more lofty in thought than many skilfully elaborated compositions; and here, too, he assuredly foresaw and conceived the sublime melodies which afterwards formed the groundwork of 'The Beatitudes.' For César Franck had, or rather *was,* the genius of improvisation, and no other modern organist, not excepting the most renowned executants, would bear the most distant comparison with him in this respect."

Much to the surprise of the composer himself, as well as of his friends, who understood his utter inability to use the political arts necessary to insure institutional preferment, Franck was appointed Professor of Organ at the Conservatoire in 1872.

III

"The Beatitudes"

He had already been at work some time on "The Beatitudes," a labor which he now interrupted to make a musical setting of "The Redemption." After scanty rehearsals, this oratorio was given a perfunctory performance at a "Concert Spirituel" in Passion Week, 1872. For the next six years (making ten years in all) every moment which Franck could give to composition was devoted to "The Beatitudes," which were eventually completed in 1879.

His naïveté.

Feeling that this work was his *magnum opus*, Franck naively hoped to interest the directors of the Conservatoire and other powers in musical officialdom by giving a first performance at his house for their benefit. Unfortunately the great men felt they had more important business elsewhere. But few besides his pupils were present, and of the "important guests" two only remained to hear the end of the music. Even the ingenuous Franck was somewhat daunted by this reception of his masterpiece, and was persuaded by his friends to divide the work into eight portions, hoping that parts of it, at least, might arrive at public performance. It was not until fourteen years later, three years after Franck's death, that the work was given in its entirety for the first time in public at a Colonne concert.

Honored as a "professor."

Perhaps it was as an attempt at compensation for this slight that the Government bestowed on Franck shortly afterward the purple ribbon of an Officer of the Academy, an inferior rank, which was raised some years later to that of Chevalier of the Legion of Honor. Unfortunately, the artist's gratification at this tardy recognition was tempered by the fact that it was bestowed on the "professor" and not on the "composer."

As a sympathetic exploitation of him as a composer, his friends and pupils gave a concert entirely of his works at the Cirque d'Hiver in the season of 1886-87. The pieces were so inadequately given that no one but the composer himself was satisfied; but he, very characteristically, told his friends: "You are really too exacting; for my own part, I was quite satisfied."

Purity of his aims.

Two years later, February 17, 1889, his Symphony was given for the first time by the Société des Concerts du Conservatoire. The audience, including the critics, were bewildered by its novelty and individuality; but when Franck, on his return home, was asked by his anxious family, "Did the public like it? Was there plenty of applause?" he answered with a beaming smile of content, "Oh, it sounded well, just as I thought it would."

IV

His later years.

Franck's last years were made happy by the success of his violin sonata, played by Eugène Ysaye all over the world, and by the unprecedented ovation given him on the performance of his string quartet at the concert of the Société Nationale, April 19, 1890. This first taste of popular appreciation came to him late, in his sixty-ninth year, but long neglect had not embittered him, and he received the plaudits with a pleased surprise, saying to the group of friends about him, "There, you see, the public is beginning to understand me."

And death.

Unfortunately, he did not live long to bask in the sunlight of his tardy triumph. A month later, on his way to give a lesson, in crossing the street, he was struck by the pole of a wagon. The accident proved more serious than was at first thought. He gradually failed in health, and, complications setting in, died at his home, November 8, 1890. In spite of his increasing weakness during these last weeks he worked at his compositions to the end. The three beautiful Chorals, his swan song, lay beside him on his bed when the priest came to give him the consolations of the Church.

Love of his disciples.

No more fitting close to a sketch of the life of this singularly pure-hearted artist could be found than the last words of the funeral oration, delivered at his grave by Emmanuel Chabrier in the name of the Société Nationale de Musique: "Farewell, Master, and take our thanks, for you have done well. In you, we salute one of the greatest artists of the century, and also the incomparable teacher whose wonderful work has produced a whole generation of forceful musicians. . . . We salute, also, the upright and just man, so humane, so distinguished, whose counsels were sure, as his words were kind. Farewell!"

Prélude, Choral, et Fugue, for piano (published in the Litolff Edition).

Example for analysis, No. 19.

This work has been selected for analysis here in spite of its difficulty both of performance and of comprehension, because it is not on the whole more difficult that Franck's other great composition for the piano, the "Prélude, Aria, et Final," and because it is a splendid example of his finest qualities as a composer. His curiously chromatic style of melody and harmony, perhaps the most original of all his traits, is seen at its best in the choral, and underlies also the eloquence of the beautiful fugue. The latter illustrates again his marvelous contrapuntal skill, his ability to weave melodies together, not with academic science, but with living emotion. And finally the masterly construction of the entire work, making a single organic unit of its many elements, illustrates that constructive power of Franck which was, in degree if not in kind, almost unique among modern composers, and which his pupil, M. d'Indy, has made an accessible influence for all future musicians by his treatise on musical composition.

In the same author's biography of his teacher he tells us that in 1884 "César Franck, struck by the lack of serious works [for piano], set to work with a youthful fervor which belied his sixty years to try if he could not adopt the old æsthetic forms to the new technique of the piano, a problem which could only be solved by some considerable modifications in the externals of these forms.

"In the Prélude, Choral, et Fugue all is new both as regards invention and workmanship. . . . Franck started with the intention of simply writing a prelude and fugue in the style of Bach, but he soon took up the idea of linking these two movements together by a chorale, the melodic spirit of which should brood over the whole work. Thus it came about that he produced a work which was purely personal, but in which none of the constructive details were left to chance or improvisation; on the contrary, the materials all serve, without exception, to contribute to the beauty and solidity of the structure."

Prélude. The tonality is B, a key of which César Franck was especially fond, both in the minor and in the major mode. The main theme (see Figure XIa) is at once given out, surrounded by an arpeggio accompaniment figure that recalls the style of Bach's organ preludes. Soon a rhapsodic passage, marked "a capriccio," forecasts the fundamental theme of the entire work, which at present, however, is only suggested (Figure XIb; the characteristic motive of three notes, in this as in later excerpts, is indicated by a bracket).

Figure XI

THE PRELUDE.

(*a*) **Main theme of Prelude.**

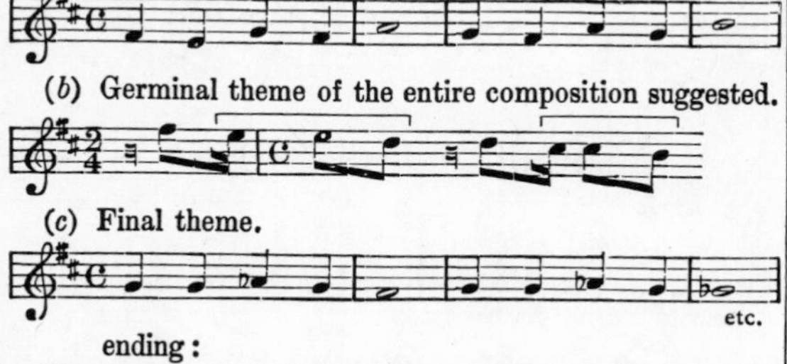

The same two elements next appear in the dominant key of F sharp minor, the first at the bottom of page 3, the second in the last measure on page 4. This is developed at some

CHAP. XI

length before it leads back to the original key and to a third, and concluding, theme almost identical with the first (Figure XIc).

Choral. "The Choral," says M. d'Indy, "in three parts, oscillating between E flat minor and C minor, displays two distinct elements: a superb and expressive phrase which foreshadows and prepares the way for the subject of the Fugue, and the choral proper, of which the three prophetic words—if we may so call them—roll forth in sonorous volutions, in a serene, religious majesty."

The first section presents the phrase suggestive of the fugue theme, asserting once more the motive underlying the work as a whole

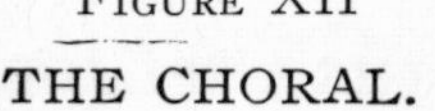

FIGURE XII

THE CHORAL.

Figure XIIa). The intensely chromatic Franckian style of the harmony will be noted.

The first "word" of the choral proper, as M. d'Indy so felicitously calls it, starts at the eleventh measure, and is noble indeed with its steady rhythmic march, its strong diatonic melody and bass (contrasting finely with the chromatic style of the other sections) and its voluminous organ-like chords. It is this time delivered pianissimo, and in C minor (see Figure XIIb).

The third section presents another phrase, somewhat similar to the first, and like it referring to the basic motive (Figure XIIc). It modulates from C minor to the subdominant, F minor, where the second "word" is proclaimed (page 8, bottom line).

A fifth section, intensely chromatic like both the other contrasts, suggests a slight variation on the central motive, which is nevertheless, still recognizable (Figure XIId). During this section there is an impressive climax, preparing the way for the final triumphant assertion of the "word," in the tonic key, E flat minor.

Fugue. Two pages of rhapsodic matter, suggesting improvisation, but never letting the central thought be really forgotten, lead over to the key of B minor, in which the Fugue starts, at the bottom of page 11, with the first announcement of the complete theme so long held, so to speak, in solution (Figure XIIIa). The "answer," in F sharp minor, comes at the top of page 12. A third voice takes up the subject in the ninth measure of this page, and a fourth (the bass) in the thirteenth. An episode fills the lower half of the page. Further entrances in A major and D major (page 13) lead to a gradual accession of energy until at the end of the fourth line the subject is stated with great vigor in A major. The force then again abates, and a quiet cadence is reached in D major.

Figure XIII

THE FUGUE.

With the fourth measure on page 14 begins a statement of the theme *inverted* (Figure XIIIb), followed immediately by a second statement to the same effect, both in the bass. This inverted form, despite its melodic and harmonic interest, is however abandoned, after these two sporadic appearances, in favor of an episode which, although it commences, to be sure, very softly, nevertheless begins to build up a new excitement by its more agitated rhythm of triplets in eighth notes. All through pages 15 and 16 the climactic movement progresses, intensified by various entrances of the theme in its original inflection downwards, until with the splendidly sonorous entrance on page 17 comes the acme, followed by a pause and a sort of cadenza bringing back the rhythm of the Prélude. This prepares the way for a reaffirmation of the chief theme (the "word") of the Choral, pronounced climactically, on pages 19 and 20, in B minor, G minor, and E flat minor (incomplete), and so leading back to the main tonality of B minor, where, at the bottom of page 20, comes the apotheosis in which are combined all the parts of the work. The Prélude is represented by the rhythm of its accompaniment; the "word" theme from the Choral is heard not only in the treble but also, making a canon, in the bass; and the most important theme of all, that of the Fugue, enters in the last measure on the page. After the attendant developments, the work closes with a jubliant announcement of the choral theme in the major.

CHAPTER XII

Peter Ilyitsch Tschaïkowsky

I

Nationalism in music.

N OUR studies of Grieg and Dvořák we have observed how the folk-music of remote countries long retains peculiarities of interval and of rhythm, obliterated in more sophisticated music; how these peculiarities in their quaintness and unfamiliarity bring a fresh delight to jaded ears; and how exploiters of them have made artistic capital of this fact by cultivating, in many countries, the musical specialty known as nationalism. Sometimes, as notably in the case of Dvořák, the process has been unconscious and inevitable. In other cases, of which Grieg's is a striking example, nationalism has been adopted consciously and after reaching "years of discretion." In the latter instance its results have not been altogether happy; it has often tended to make artistic expression narrower, rather than broader, with the passing of years; and Grieg is not the only composer whom, in the phrase of Mr. Frederick Niecks, it has "prevented from forming a style by imposing on him a manner." Such nationalism, like the patriotism it reflects, may be a loyalty so narrow as to be in effect disloyal to wider, humaner ideals. And on the other hand eclecticism, however disastrous when adopted negatively, through cowardice or conventionality, may be, when espoused with vigor, conviction and enthusiasm, a far safer and finer attitude of mind, and minister to an essentially higher type of art.

These considerations may help us to understand why it is that, as representatives of a country so musically remote, peculiar, even semi-barbarous as Russia, a country whose folk-song has to an almost unrivaled degree the quaintness and freshness to European ears that reside in modal intervals and uneven rhythms, such nationalists as Moussorgsky and Balakirev are still accepted only by students and specialists, while the Russian whose music is loved all over the world is Tschaïkowsky, the "eclectic." Here is a paradox worth investigating.

The "New Russian" school.

The nationalist contemporaries of Tschaïkowsky formed a brilliant group, organized under the name of the "New Russian" School, of which Mily Balakirev (born 1836) was the "guide, philosopher and friend." In spite of their artistic differences, it may be noted that Tschaïkowsky was on terms of cordial personal friendship with Balakirev, as well as with some of his disciples. These were Nicolas Rimsky-Korsakoff (1844-1908), composer of the delightful Scheherezade suite and of many operas; Modeste Petrovich Moussorgsky (1839-1886), the undisciplined genius who wrote the extraordinarily powerful opera, Boris Godounoff; Alexander Borodine (1834-1887), chemist, inventor, philanthropist, as well as composer of one of the finest of modern symphonies, unduly neglected; and César Cui (1835-..), military engineer and critic. Cui has formulated the tenets of the "New School," so far as concerns operatic composition, in which all Russian composers, including Tschaïkowsky, have been especially interested, as follows:

Tenets of the "New School."

"1. Commonplaces are as unbearable in the opera as in symphonic music.

"2. The music must follow the dramatic situation, step by step, whence greater liberty and diversity of forms.

"3. The book must be, as far as possible, a literary and poetic work, and must not be disfigured by the music. On the contrary, the music, closely bound to the text, constituting with it a unity, must draw from it a new and double force of expression, this exacting supple and irreproachable declamation.

"4. The character of the personages must be brought forth in strong relief."

To these explicit principles may be added the use of Russian folk-song, either in literal quotation or in modified use of idiom, which is a fundamental practice with these composers.

CHAP. XII

As the first point, about commonplaces, is little more than a truism, except in so far as it may have some implicit meaning not revealed with sufficient clearness for discussion, we may dismiss it with the remark that Tschaïkowsky is not so afraid of commonplaces as are his fellow-countrymen of the New School. Indeed, he no more fears them or goes out of his way to avoid them than does Schubert, Haydn, Handel, or even his idol, Mozart. He is no musical *précieux*. His attitude toward style is not that of Pater or Wilde, but that of Dickens, Thackeray or Fielding. Like other great men, he can be distressingly banal.

Tschaïkowsky and the new school.

The second, third and fourth points, insisting, as they do, on objective expression, subservience of music to text, and minute characterization, proceed obviously from the Berlioz-Liszt tradition, with its emphasis always on the dramatic and the pictorial, and do violence at every step to the temperament of Tschaïkowsky, who was as subjective a musician as ever lived. Tschaïkowsky wrote music to voice his own feelings, simply, often naïvely, sometimes almost hysterically, and had neither the patience nor the emotional detachment requisite to "follow the dramatic situation, step by step." For sincerity, directness, unsophistication in expression, he belongs with Schubert and Dvořák; he has both the strength and the weakness of that type.

Subjectivity.

The same limitations, the obverse of glorious musical qualities, show in his inability to

CHAP. XII

characterize minutely and in detail. Mrs. Newmarch, in her interesting criticism of his most popular opera, Eugene Oniegin, points out that "the characters in the story offer several strongly marked contrasts, of which Tschaïkowsky has not availed himself in his musical presentment of them." She attributes the great success of the work chiefly to the fact that "Tschaïkowsky has attuned himself without difficulty to the subjective and sentimental mood of the poet, which was so often his most characteristic temper of mind." And she sums up by quoting Berezovsky to the effect that this opera "is like a woman with many faults of heart and character, but whom we love for her beauty in spite of them all."

More a musician than a poet.

But it is in his treatment of his texts and in his generally skeptical attitude toward the dogma of subservience of music to text that he gives most convincing evidence of what music means to him—subjective expression rather than illustration. His best songs are those, like the celebrated "Nur wer die Sehnsucht kennt" and the beautiful Invocation to Sleep, in which he makes no effort after a meticulous appropriateness of each note to each syllable, but writes a broad melody, steeped in the sentiment of melancholy, wistful or passionate, which was his natural mood. Like Schubert, he was far from conscientious about declamation, far from fastidious in the choice of texts; even Schubert would have been scandalized by his interpolations in the finest texts of such convenient exclamations as

"Good Heavens!" "Alas!" "Woe is me!" M. Cui wittily remarks that "the union of the two arts [poetry and music] appeared to Tschaïkowsky in the light of a *mésalliance* for the one he represented."

Dislikes recitative.

His attitude toward recitative, as it is revealed in his criticism of Dargomijsky's The Stone Guest, is characteristic. "His strength lay," says Tschaïkowsky, "exclusively in his wonderful realism and in his eminently vocal recitative. . . . The composer recognized the dominant quality of his gift; but this . . . led him to the strange notion of composing an opera consisting entirely of recitative. . . . We know that recitative has no definite rhythm, no clearly defined melody or musical form—it is merely the cement which unites the various parts of a musical edifice. What an aberration of a daring mind! . . . To write an opera without music—is not this the same as writing a drama without words or action?" "Opera without music"—Tschaïkowsky tacitly assumes here, in obedience to his temperament, that "music" is lyric melody, that is, the expression of subjective emotion. We need not be surprised at his rejection of the dramatico-pictorial conception of music of the New School. Even one of its own members, Borodine, in many respects the most musical of them all, has made the confession: "I have always disagreed with a great number of my friends concerning dramatic music. Recitative is not in my nature: I am attracted rather by melody. I am more and more in favor of complete and concrete forms. In opera, as in decorative art, details are not in place; only great lines are needed."

II

His eclecticism.

This instinctive preference of subjective emotion and plastic beauty to characterization, innate in Tschaïkowsky, as to some extent in Borodine, is the key which unlocks the often discussed mysteries of his attitude toward folk-music. The native music of Russia, despite the fascination it exercised over him as a Russian, was too strictly circumscribed, both in expression and in structural interest, to satisfy a heart and mind that were not only Russian, but human. That he was far from indifferent to it he has shown in such compositions as the well-known Andante of his early string quartet in D and the second symphony; but that he could not be confined within so narrow an idiom he showed by the entire trend of his later work, as well as by the wide eclecticism of his tastes as revealed in his critical writings. His loving appreciation of Mozart is shown in all that he says of him, and, better still, in his delightful "Mozartiana" orchestral suite. "The glamor and warmth of the South," Mrs. Newmarch tells us, "so forcibly expressed by Rossini's brilliant dramatic power, exercised the strongest fascination for . . . this northern composer." And so subjective a nature could not but be strongly sympathetic with the most *innig* of all composers, Schumann, by whom he was

A lover of Mozart.

deeply influenced. Tschaïkowsky, in short, was admirably free from that artistic egoism which leads a composer to shut himself up, so to speak, in a glass case, either personal or national, for fear his individuality may escape; he believed, rather, in a perfectly free assimilation of all contemporary influences; and few candid critics who will take the trouble to examine, for instance, his series of six symphonies, stretching from his youth to the very end of his life, will regret the gradual universalizing of his style which carried him from the Russianism of the second to the humanity of the "Pathétique."

Yet at heart Slavonic.

Yet, however "eclectic," in the best sense, a composer's style may become, it remains, of course, true that some of his most fundamental qualities of temperament will always remain racial, or even national, and that consequently a study of the native music of his people may call our attention to basic elements in his more developed art which, without it, we should miss or undervalue. Such is the case with Tschaïkowsky. For all his cosmopolitanism, he is at the core Slavonic. Let us see, then, what are the main peculiarities of the Russian folk-song.

III

Peculiarities of Russian folk-music.

First of all, it retains, like the Bohemian and the Norwegian, certain modal intervals which through the influence of harmony have died out in our modern scales, notably the flattened seventh scale-step ("leading-tone"), which destroys the sense of finality in the common cadence, and gives often the feeling rather of a half-close on the dominant. This gives a sense of inconclusiveness, of vacillating indecision, which is strangely suggestive of that weakness of will which Turgenev's novels reveal as a basic Russian trait. The effect is well shown in the second and fourth phrases of the melody in Figure XIVa, taken from Rimsky-Korsakoff's collection of one hundred Russian folk-songs.

Figure XIV

Even more curious is the cadence of the first and third phrases—a fall from the fourth step of the scale to the keynote (4-1) of indescribable melancholy and charm. This cadence is perhaps the most Russian feature of Russian folk-music. We find it everywhere. Those who heard the Russian Balalaïka Orchestra play the Song of the Volga Boatman are not likely to forget the haunting sadness of its recurrence, as if the singer, under some baleful spell, wandered endlessly in a circle of four notes (Figure XIVb). Tschaïkowsky bases the introduction of his second and most national symphony on an elegiac horn theme in which it is conspicuous (Figure XIVc). It also appears, as we shall see in a moment, in the tune on which the Andante of his first string quartet is founded.

The monotonous repetition of short phrases, exemplified in the Volga Boat Song, is likewise found in most of the tunes, whether sad or gay, and gives to sadness a despair, and to joy a feverish fury, which are alike semi-barbarous. Mr. Granville Bantock, in his collection of One Hundred Folk-Songs from All Nations,* mentions not only this insistence on single melodic phrases, but the ingenuity by which its monotony is often rendered endurable, and even interesting, by varying the harmony at each recurrence.† The student can hardly fail to note the analogy of certain highly characteristic passages in Tschaïkowsky, such as the endless iterations of a two-

*The Musicians' Library, Oliver Ditson Company.

†Examples will be found in the National Album of Russian Melodies in the Peters Edition, pp. 22 and 24.

measure phrase over the pedal point D monotonously tapped on the kettle-drum in the slow movement of the Pathétique Symphony (small score, page 96; piano score, two hands, Pachulsky, page 34).

Finally, the singular ease and fluency with which the composer treats the five-beat measure in this movement may remind us that the Russian as well as the Bohemian mind shows a debonair irresponsibility in its dealings with measure that is probably a general Slavonic trait, and is certainly in marked contrast with the stricter accentual morality of the Teuton. Arensky's Studies in Forgotten Rhythms are only extreme instances of an interest in flexible metre that is normally strong in all Slavs, and has enabled them to contribute to modern technique an enrichment not easily exaggerated.

Example for analysis, No. 20. Andante cantabile, from the String Quartet in D, opus 11. (Transcribed for piano by Ch. Klindworth.)

The main theme, sixteen measures long, a folk-song brought to Tschaïkowsky's attention by the singing of a plasterer working on his house, figures as number 14 in Rimsky-Korsakoff's collection. Unlike the songs we have so far considered in being in major rather than in minor mode, it yet has the main Russian hall-marks: the 4-1 cadence in the first and third phrases; the final close on the dominant, inconclusively; and the metric irregularity of the mixed measures of two and three beats, or, in Rimsky-Korsakoff's notation, of four and five (see Figure XV). Its treatment by Tschaïkowsky, who was a skilled contrapuntist, consists largely, it will be seen, of attractive imitations of the opening figure.

A second melody, in D-flat major, original and exceedingly graceful, is accompanied by one of those persistent rhythmic figures, entrusted in this case to the 'cello, to which the composer is addicted.

Figure XV

The main theme recurs, treated now precisely as Rimsky-Korsakoff treats it, at first in two-part counterpoint, later in expressive though rather severe harmony. Tschaïkowsky was evidently familiar with his colleague's collection—or was the latter made after his quartet was written?

The secondary theme is sung once more (on the G-string) with a piquantly rhythmed accompaniment, and a brief coda on the folk-motive ends this deservedly popular piece.

IV

Life and character.

Peter Ilyitch Tschaïkowsky, born April 25, 1840, approached music, like so many other Russian composers, as an amateur, intending at first to make the law his profession. When he was twenty-one he wrote his sister that he was considering becoming a musician, but was doubtful whether he could succeed. "Perhaps idleness may take possession of me, and I may not persevere." The remark reflects a timidity, a lack of self-confidence that haunted him even to his latest years, as we see in the Life and Letters edited by his brother; as a matter of fact, he was a model of industry and system in all his work. From 1866 to 1877 he was professor of harmony in the Moscow Conservatory; but teaching was always uncongenial to his high-strung temperament, and after the nervous breakdown which followed his unhappy marriage became intolerable to him. Fortunately, he was enabled by the munificence of Frau von Meck, the widow of a wealthy engineer, to devote himself entirely to composing from 1878 on. His fourth symphony, dedicated to her, was the first fruit of her generous and delicately bestowed patronage, and most of his finest works belong to the fifteen years from this time to his death in 1893.

An unbalanced nervous system.

The morbid hypersensitiveness of the nervous system from which Tschaïkowsky suffered all his life, which made each mood as it came to him so vivid that he could see no other, and thus underlay his extreme subjectivism and his tendency to exaggerate, is what ultimately explains his strength and his weakness, both as a man and as an artist. He is emotional almost to hysteria; he deals in unrelated extremes; mediation, relation, balance, and their artistic correlatives of restraint and proportion, are not only unattainable, but distasteful to him, as is shown by his unavailing efforts to like the music of Brahms. His lack of reticence, his habit of "wearing his heart on his sleeve," as Mrs. Newmarch puts it, "in a very graceful, and not too unmanly fashion," while it has won him great popularity, prevents him from attaining the noble dignity of more reserved spirits, of Brahms, Beethoven, or Bach. Indeed, while his breadth of mind led him, as we have seen, to grow away from and beyond the letter of the Russian folk-music as he grew older, his emotions remained always a little barbaric, and Mr. Edward Dannreuther's characterization of his art, "Fiery exaltation on a basis of languid melancholy," is in essence as applicable to the Symphonie Pathétique, his most mature and personal work, as it is to his much more idiomatically Russian second symphony, or even to the folk-music itself.

"Exaltation on a basis of melancholy."

The "fiery exaltation" shows not only in the truly barbaric noisiness of the Overture 1812, but much more admirably in those long, relentless, cumulative climaxes with which he knows how to play on our nerves as a hypnotist plays on his subject. The march movement of the Pathétique is one of the most brilliant things in modern music, not only in orchestration, but in conception. But the basis of his art, as Mr. Dannreuther states, is not fiery exaltation, but the "languid melancholy," ever smouldering, out of which it leaps flame-like when blown upon by passion. That mood of melancholy, however it may be qualified by others, we cannot but take to be the essential Tschaïkowsky. Its evidences are found in his peculiar mannerisms and methods on almost every page. His songful, earnest, largely diatonic melody, in spite of its occasionally Italian suavity, emanates usually from a sincere and heartfelt sadness. His insistence on a reiterated rhythm is the insistence of the melancholic victim of a fixed idea. His wonderful use of low registers, as at the beginning and the end of the Pathétique, perhaps his most original contribution to the resources of expression, is eloquent of sinister foreboding, of dull pain and despair.

Example for analysis, No. 21. Finale of the Symphonie Pathétique. (Pachulsky's edition for two hands.)

The poignancy of the main theme, a simple diatonic melody, is greatly enhanced by the chromatic coloring given by the harmonization. Note the rising sequence in measures 5 ff, and the expressiveness of the interlinked suspensions. On the repetition of the theme, this sequence descends (with striking alteration of expressive quality), and ends with an extraordinary descent of the bassoon into the lowest regions.

Against a pulsating accompaniment of horns the first violins and violas now sing the tender and noble second theme, repeated several times with growing intensity and culminating in a turmoil of the full orchestra and a dramatic silence. Presently the first theme returns, at first simply, but soon, in the remarkable passage beginning at the top of page 70, made the subject of one of those irresistible slow climaxes already mentioned. Notice the steady, implacable rise of the trombones and bassoon up the scale from the middle of the page. This leads into the overpowering reëntrance of the main theme over a pedal point of F-sharp, and commented upon by the savage stopped note of the horn, which no one who has heard the symphony can ever forget. With this outburst the music spends its passion, and after solemn trombone harmonies (top of page 72) the second theme reënters in B minor, grievous and detached, as if commenting on a tragedy already removed to another world, and sinking lower and lower to the deepest register, pulsates more and more slowly and hesitantly until it falls to silence.

CHAPTER XIII

Johannes Brahms

I

The "three B's."

THE peculiar position of Brahms in the history of music is, on the whole, not inaptly described by the frequently heard phrase that he is "the last of the great classical German school." Considerable as are the romantic and even the impressionistic elements in his work, as seen, for instance, in the later piano pieces and in songs like the "Lerchengesang," in fundamental mood he stands sharply opposed to the sensuousness of Wagnerism, and preserves the older earnestness and large simplicity of Bach and Beethoven, with whom he has been bracketed in von Bülow's oft-repeated remark about "The Three B's." He was wholly immune to the Berlioz-Liszt theatricalism, which infected so many of his lesser contemporaries. As for his followers, Strauss is the only one who can be compared with him in natural endowment, and Strauss is both too sentimental and too sensational to be called in any significant sense classic. Reger, who shares Brahms's admiration for Bach and his keen instinct for the polyphonic, is too much the schoolmaster to rise to equal artistic heights—he is in the last analysis lacking in the profound human emotion which almost always vitalizes Brahms's intellectual profundity.

In what sense is Brahms classic?

Brahms is classic, then, in the same sense that Bach and Beethoven are classic, in that his attitude toward life, expressed in his art, is simple, large, broad, free from the feverish passion and the exaggeration and lack of balance which are the characteristic defects of romanticism. Just as Sir Hubert Parry finds in Beethoven "the perfect balance of expression and design," so we may suggest the quality of Brahms by saying that in him deep emotion is controlled by masterful intelligence. To accuse him of lack of feeling is to expose one's own superficiality; but to say that intelligence is more obvious to a first hearing of his music than feeling is perhaps true; or we may say that Brahms *feels intellectually,* like all musicians of reflective temperament, and that his music, therefore, reveals its full meaning only after repeated hearings and attentive study. This sober and yet mellow thoughtfulness of mood is Brahms's essential characteristic: it underlies not only his whole attitude toward life and art, but even the minute peculiarities, the technical mannerisms of his work.

II

Characteristic methods.

It finds its natural melodic expression, for instance, in those simple, almost naïve tunes, moving along the scale or made up from the tones of the common chord, which Brahms, like Beethoven, has created on the model of German folk-song. The family resemblance of the chief themes of Beethoven's Eroica, Fifth, and Eighth Symphonies, and of Brahms's Second Symphony, Violin Concerto, and Sapphic Ode, all descended from the common ancestor, Do-mi-sol, is too striking to require comment. The plain dignity of the diatonic scale is the foundation of Brahms's music, as it is of Beethoven's, Haydn's, Handel's and Bach's. The chromatic element he uses often with great poignancy, but always as subordinate. His art touches that of his greatest contemporary on the Meistersinger side, not the Tristan and Isolde.

A genius in rhythm.

His intellectual subtlety, on the other hand, much greater than the emotional, shows itself in an elaboration and complication of the rhythmic element of music probably unmatched in any other composer. The breadth and flexibility of his phrases are extraordinary; each sings itself out to its natural end with the noble deliberation of inexhaustible fecundity; and though balance is always secured, it is always large and free, never the sing-song squareness of the small imagination. The prosody of the songs may be studied for illustration. Interesting combinations of two notes to the beat with three are everywhere in Brahms, and his oppositions of metrical and rhythmical accents, through the shifting of short figures in the measure, are endlessly ingenious. The distaste for obvious dispositions, to be sure, sometimes leads him to artificial displacements, such as result in the "hobbling rhythm," which Mr. Weingartner describes as a mannerism*; his formulæ do occasionally smell of the lamp; but these defects are insignificant indeed compared with the remarkable contribution he has made to the growth of rhythm.†

Thematic development.

The same wealth of imagination is shown in his thematic development, of which he is incontestably one of the greatest masters, if not the greatest, since Beethoven. Like Beethoven, he is fond of starting out a large work with one or two brief fragments of motive (the chief motive of his second symphony, like that of Beethoven's fifth, consisting of but four notes) and evolving from it undreamt-of interest. This will be illustrated in detail in our second example for analysis. His presentation of still further and unexpected developments in the coda may be traced back to the same prototype; his codas are justly famous for their fascinating surprises and unforeseen fulfilments, such as are illustrated, for example, in the first movement

*Felix Weingartner: The Symphony Since Beethoven.

†See The Rhythm of Modern Music, by C. F. Abdy Williams, Chapters V, VIII and IX.

of the E minor 'Cello Sonata, the A major Piano Quartet, the second symphony.

His music is "better than it sounds."

So completely is he thus immersed in his musical thought that there is a certain truth in the criticism charging him with indifference to sensuous effect. The witticism that Tschaikowsky's music sounds better than it is, while Brahms's is better than it sounds, calls our attention to the fact that with the German the thought comes first, instead of modifying itself to suit sonorities and technique. "What a relief," said a musician after hearing his second symphony for the first time for several years, "that Brahms always says what he means, instead of what will 'come off' well! It makes his music last." Undoubtedly his contempt for effect for its own sake makes him write some dull, gray, heavy pages; his strings sometimes lack brilliancy, and the finale of his first 'cello sonata is a standing evidence of what discomfort he will inflict on the ear when misled by an academic ambition. But, on the other hand, no one has conceived ideas more inevitably incarnated in a certain tonal color. Listen to the wonderful horn tune that starts off the Trio, opus 40, or the melody in which the flute speaks so heroically in the finale of the First Symphony, or the Intermezzo for piano, opus 76, No. 3, and then try to deny Brahms the color sense! Such a conductor as Mr. Weingartner may in a snapshot judgment call Brahms's orchestra austere, but on further acquaintance he writes a whole article to prove that the composer's colors are the necessary ones for the expression of his ideas. Amateurs call his piano music *unklaviermässig*—unsuited to the piano—but thoughtful artists like Mr. Harold Bauer hold that he has created a new idiom for the piano, free from empty bravura, large and massive and noble like himself.

III

Youth and early work.

Johannes Brahms, born in Hamburg on May 7, 1833, was the son of an orchestral contrabass player, and was trained for music as a matter of course from his earliest years. He made a concert tour as a pianist with the violinist Remenyi, taking along his early compositions; he met Liszt, and did not get on with him; he was greeted by Schumann as the coming genius, the "chosen youth, over whose cradle the Graces and the Heroes seem to have kept watch." At this time he was a tow-haired, smooth-faced youth of twenty, stocky and vigorous, with blue eyes of great liquidity and depth, and a still boyishly soprano voice. No wonder the romanticist Schumann was delighted with the piano pieces he brought with him—the three sonatas, op. 1, 2 and 5, and the Scherzo, opus 4. The torrential enthusiasm of youth, which foams through them, must have carried him away. And with it there is a tender limpidity in the quieter passages, like the second theme of the F minor Sonata, and a large seriousness, as in the Andante of the same work, that was both true to the best German tradition and characteristic of the maturer Brahms to come. There was also, rather curiously, a tendency to use specific programs, or to illustrate poetic ideas, which is in direct opposition to the composer's later practice. In these early pieces he was feeling his way; their turgidity and waywardness he later completely outgrew; yet there may be noted in them, in germ, all the more characteristic qualities of his mature work.

Example for analysis, No. 22. Ballade, opus 10, No. 1 after the Scottish ballad, "Edward."

The "program" is suggested by a well-known ballad in Percy's Reliques, known to Brahms through Herder's translation. The first stanza of the original reads:

"'Why dais your brand [i.e., sword] sae drap wi bluid,
Edward, Edward?
Why dais your brand sae drap wi bluid,
And why sae sad gang yee O?'
'O I hae killed my hawk sae guid,
Mither, Mither!
O I hae killed my hawk sae guid,
And I had nae mair bot hee O.'"

As the dialogue proceeds, the mother forces from her son the confession that he has killed his father. This tragic and at the same time remote, mediæval and legendary atmosphere Brahms has suggested with remarkable power.

The opening phrase, in D minor, with its repeated falling cadence on the dominant, is based precisely, it will be noted, on the rhythm of the opening lines with their monotonous refrain, "Edward, Edward." The lengthening of the responsive phrase, suggested by the poem, illustrates Brahms's flexible sense of rhythm. In the *poco più moto,* again (Edward's reply), we have an example of his rhythmic subtlety: the phrase is five beats in length; being repeated four times, it shifts each time its relation to the measure, commencing first on a fourth beat, then on a first, then on a second, and finally on a third. It is such details, small but far from insignificant, that give Brahms's music its rhythmic vitality. After the mother's couplet has been heard again the *poco più mosso* recurs with singular and, perhaps at first, unanalyzable charm. It will soon be perceived that the melody is an *inversion* of the first one: it moves by the same intervals, just reversed in direction; thus imaginatively does Brahms employ an academic device in the service of a poetic idea. As regards the general style of this section, the student will notice the diatonic, almost folk-like character of the melody, and the simplicity, yet expressiveness, of the harmony. The open fifths, without thirds, in two of the cadences, suggest the very mood of the text—a sadness touched with the sense of the uncanny.

The middle Allegro, in D major, takes the shape of a slow, relentless and powerful climax, depicting the agitation and terror of Edward's confession. Musically, it is a good example of Brahms's power of thematic development, of making much from little. It all comes from the first five notes in the bass,

Chap. XIII

constituting a motive which in turn is derived from the beginning of the second *poco più moto* described above. The excitement, and at the same time the sustained power of the whole passage depends not a little on the rhythm of three against two so often used by the composer. Note that as the passion increases, the motive shortens to three notes. The climax culminates in a fortissimo repetition, in the fullest and boldest sonorities of Brahms's massive piano style, of Edward's theme, which gradually expends its force and dies away in an impressive diminuendo.

Now returns the first tempo and theme, ornamented this time with a subordinate triplet rhythm (beginning with a silence—notice the impressiveness of that); and the piece ends with the low, gloomy harmonies appropriate.

IV

Later life and work.

After the acclamation by Schumann came a lull in Brahms's life, a time in which he analyzed anew his ideals, modified them in important respects, and finally embarked on the process of development which went on unbroken for the remaining forty-odd years of his life. These years were outwardly uneventful, save for the well-deserved honors they brought. Thoreau's statement that "our thoughts are the events of our lives" was never better exemplified than in Brahms. The real interest of his life—and it is a thrilling one—is to be found in the patient and steady artistic progress he made toward the largely conceived ideal adopted when the romantic fervor of youth gave way to maturity. "Henceforth," says Dr. Deiters, "we find him striving after moderation, endeavoring to place himself more in touch with the public, and to conquer all subjectiveness. To arrive at perspicuity and precision of invention, clear design and form, careful elaboration and accurate balancing of effect, now became with him essential and established principles." In other words, Brahms left waywardness behind him, and sought to deepen, steady and universalize his feeling. By so doing he "came into his own"; and it is not in the turgid early works, but in the four noble symphonies, in the thoughtful chamber music of his middle life, and in the deeply contemplative later songs and piano pieces, that we find the essential Brahms.

Artistic ideals.

How exacting he was with himself in this lifelong artistic discipline may be gathered from such significant facts as that he wrote a contrapuntal exercise every day, that he issued a thoroughly overhauled edition of his Trio, opus 8,* or that he had his first symphony in hand ten years. In criticising one of Mr. Henschel's songs, he said: "Whether it is beautiful also is an entirely different matter, but perfect it must be"; and Sir Charles Stanford reports a similar saying, to the effect that though we cannot write as freshly

And discipline.

*The first edition exists, and may profitably be compared with the final one by the student of composition.

as Mozart, we must write as purely. It is only necessary to remember that he exacted the same high standards of others that he applied to himself in order to understand his reputation for severity amounting to "bearishness." The anecdotes illustrating this trait are legion. To a mediocre composer, who deprecated his severe criticism, saying: "But, master, if you censure me so much, I shall wish to stop composing," he replied, "Yes, that is exactly what one doesn't say to one's self often enough." To a lady who asked him which of his songs she should sing, he answered: "My posthumous ones." When incompetence was coupled with pretense, it aroused his merciless contempt. Lion-hunters were especially distasteful to him. To one who asked him if he was Brahms, he replied: "Ah, you mean my brother, the composer," and sent him off over the hills in search of this fictitious relative. Of simple people, on the other hand, and especially humble ones, children and servants, he was considerate, and would put himself to inconvenience to save them trouble. He was great enough to be quite free from petty vanity. When an admirer proposed his health in a bottle of rare wine, saying: "What this Rauenthaler is among the wines, that is Brahms among the composers," he proposed, drily, "Then let's have a bottle of Bach!"

*Example for analysis, No. 23. First movement of the Symphony in D major, opus 73.**

The basses announce at once the pregnant

*Arranged for piano, two hands. Simrock Edition.

group of four notes (called motive a in Figure XVI), which contains within itself, in germ, much of the music to come. Over this the horns immediately announce a second motive (b), which, with its repetition in the third measure, has the peculiarity we have already noticed, of being, like so many of Beethoven's themes, derived from the tones of the common chord. The phrase is completed by an inversion of motive a, which is also used, in the bass, as a sort of punctuation for each

Figure XVI

phrase, in measures five, eight and twelve. The responsive phrase, measures 6-9, given out by wood-wind instruments, differs melodically from the first one, and is paralleled by the fourth, just as the first is by the third. The second phrase will be seen later to play an important part in the development. All sorts of ingenious rhythmic variations of phrases or figures will be noticed by the alert student throughout the movement, not all of which can be mentioned in detail in our analysis. For example: the cadence melody in alto in measures 18-19 gives rise by "augmentation" to the tenor melody in the next four measures. Again, from motive a is developed the soprano melody of measures 20-21 and all the succeeding passage. Three notes of this motive will be found in measure 35, and again in 41, and their augmentation at the top of the next page.

With the third measure on this page begins, in the violins, a subsidiary melody or "bridge passage," leading over to the second theme. It is a more flowing melody, but is, nevertheless, made out of motive a (see Figure XVIc). It becomes, at the eleventh measure on this page, the subject of a series of imitations, from voice to voice, building up a climax, at the end of which (p. 4, meas. 18) reappears motive a, first in its original rhythm, later in "diminution," in eighth notes (Figure XVId). A sustained diminuendo thus leads to the second theme (p. 5, meas. 6), founded on a new motive which we may call c (Figure

XVIe). This is freely evolved, and repeated at a higher register toward the bottom of the page. Its characteristic motive, anacrustic in rhythm (leading from a weak up to the strong beat), becomes more and more conspicuous all through page 6: it appears in the bass and in shifted rhythm, then shortened to the more vigorous form of an eighth note, a sixteenth and a quarter in the treble, and finally as two sixteenths and an eighth, in which guise it is pertinaciously insisted upon. In the long climax, beginning at the bottom of the page, it is combined with a shifted form of motive a. After the fortissimo thus reached there is a quieter conclusion theme (last two lines on page 7), made from the second theme with a decorative part in triplets. So much for the long, closely knit and highly varied Exposition of thematic material.

With the double bar and the second ending begins the Development, which we must also examine in detail. First of all, theme I is sounded in the key of F major by the horn, and later in B flat by the flute. A contrapuntal passage founded on the three quarter notes of the motive leads to a vigorous passage founded on the second phrase of the theme, beginning at the second line of page 9. All this is energetically contrapuntal in style, and debouches in a grandiose announcement of motive a, in various shifts of rhythm, by the trombones and the wood-wind (the ninth measure from the bottom of the page). The exciting effect of these shiftings of accent is surprising. The "diminished" or eighth-note version of the motive next comes in for a share of elaboration (top of page 10), until with the eighteenth measure on this page the flowing subsidiary theme shown in Figure XVIc displaces it. This is combined (last four measures on the page) with motive a in its original rhythm, and later (top of the next page) with motive a in diminution in the treble, combined with motive b in various rhythmic modifications in the bass. This motive now gradually gains the ascendency to carry all before it in the emphatic passage at the bottom of the page. With further slight reminders of the subsidiary melody, the turmoil subsides, and at the middle of page 12 the Development ends and the Recapitulation begins with a gracefully decorated version of the first theme.

The student will have no difficulty in analyzing this third section, which corresponds closely with the Exposition, for himself.

At the bottom of page 16 begins one of the most poetically imagined of Brahms's codas. The wood-wind instruments sound motive b over a harmony which delays the expected final cadence, and over a held dominant-seventh chord various instruments announce an inversion of the chief motive (Figure XVIf). A solo horn next dreamfully takes this up and evolves it over mysteriously changing harmonies. The cadence thus so long evaded comes at last, restfully, deliberately, at the middle of page 17, and with it a final and indescribably tranquil and lovely statement of the main theme, as if heard in retrospect or with the mind's eye of memory. Dainty staccato diminutions of motive a follow in the wood-wind (top of page 18), leading in turn to a final call from horns and trumpet of motive b, a long-held chord of D major, with swelling and diminishing drum-roll—and silence.

CHAPTER XIV

Richard Strauss

I

N SPITE of the energy of the discussion that has raged around him for years, of the world-wide reputation he has won, and of the several distinct phases through which his work has already passed, Dr. Richard Strauss has only recently turned fifty, having been born June 11, 1864, in Munich. Artistically speaking, he is still a young man; and one of his preternatural vivacity of mind may well have many surprises still awaiting us. Evidently any critical survey of his work must be tentative and subject to revision. Our aim here will be not so much to stamp him with a formula—never a very satisfactory process—as to trace the chief phases of his development thus far, and thus suggest the peculiar quality of his artistic and human personality as it is at present realized.

Early work.

The first phase was, naturally enough, the classical. Strauss's father was a professional musician, an excellent horn player, of conservative taste, and a pronounced anti-Wagnerite. Strauss himself tells us that he was "brought up in a strictly classical way," on Haydn, Mozart, and Beethoven, and that not until he was about twenty-one years old did he come strongly under the influence of the great romantic composers—Mendelssohn, Chopin, Schumann, Brahms. His early works reflect all these models. Aside from songs and piano pieces, the most important items of this "first period" are a string quartet (1881), a sonata for violoncello and piano, a serenade for wind instruments, and a concerto for violin (all of 1882-3), and in 1883-4 a concerto for horn, a symphony, and a piano quartet. The importance of even these is hardly so much a matter of intrinsic merit as of the striking picture they give us of an extraordinary talent, disciplined, yet already somewhat cramped, by admirable, but alien, models. While there is no doubt that Strauss thoroughly learned his technique by these exercises in symphonic and chamber music, there is also plenty of evidence that his active, wayward, and essentially realistic mind was as uncomfortably constricted by them as Till Eulenspiegel was by the garments of the priest in which he masqueraded. The symphony and the quartet are ideal types of art; they aim at emotion and beauty; they are to music what lyric and epic are to literature. Now, Strauss is not an idealist, nor is he in love with ideal emotion and pure beauty. He is

Chap. XIV

drawn far less to the beautiful than to the characteristic; if the Schumanns, Chopins, and Brahms's are the Wordsworths, Keats's, and Brownings of music, Strauss is rather a Meredith, a man of observation, actuality, humor—in short, not a poet, but a novelist; and therefore he was out of place as a symphonist, and never could really find himself until he turned from the symphony to the symphonic poem.

"Ardor of the intellect."

Mr. Ernest Newman, who has written the best Strauss criticism available in English,* gets to the root of the matter when he says that though "there is ardour in the writing, it is the ardour of the intellect rather than of the emotions." His is "a temperament energetic and forthright rather than warm"; he "feels it hard to squeeze a tear out of his unclouded young eyes, to make those taut, whip-cord young nerves of his quiver with emotion"; "wherever he has to sing rather than declaim, when he has to be emotional rather than intellectual, as in his slow movements, he almost invariably fails." All this is admirably descriptive, not only of the youthful Strauss, but of the essential personality back of even the mature works, as we shall see more in detail as we progress. Mr. Newman finds an exception, to be sure, in the slow movement of the Piano Quartet, opus 13, over which he becomes lyrical in praise: "This

* In his "Richard Strauss," in the Living Masters of Music series, and also in his "Musical Studies," essays on "Program Music" and on "Richard Strauss and the Music of the Future."

movement," he says, "stands unique among Strauss's work, both in its pure beauty and in its æsthetic purpose. For once in his life, at all events, the great realist has had his honeyed hour of idealism." To which we might report that there is hardly so much honey as that in genuine idealism. The chief theme of the movement is surely not free of a mawkishness, a sentimentality, that Strauss too easily lapses into when he tries for pure sentiment, as notably in the love music of "Don Juan," "Ein Heldenleben," and other works. The movement really supports, it would seem, rather than forms an exception to, the truth of Mr. Newman's theory. The only part of it in the least distinguished, the only part that rises above a rather stereotyped German "schwärmerei," is the codetta in which, with

His besetting sentimentality.

FIGURE XVII

From the Andante of Strauss's Quartet for Piano and Strings, opus 13.

its widely skipping, incisively rhythmed melodic figure, the Strauss of Till Eulenspiegel, the satyr-Strauss, gives a whisk of his tail and enlivens the drowsy, fragrance-laden summer afternoon atmosphere.

II

Strauss finds himself as a realist.

A trip to Italy in the spring of 1886, and the intellectual influence of his friend Alexander Ritter, were the chief external influences contributing to the change which in 1886 came over the youthful Strauss, and initiated what has been called his second period (1886-1894). To this time belong four symphonic poems: Aus Italien (1886), Macbeth (1886-7), Don Juan (1888), and Tod und Verklärung (Death and Transfiguration—1889). Besides many songs, he also now wrote his first opera, Guntram, and his Violin Sonata (1887), the last of the chamber music works. Of the influence of his friend Ritter the composer has himself remarked: "Alexander Ritter was exceptionally well read in all the philosophers, ancient and modern, and a man of the highest culture. His influence was like a storm wind. He urged me on to the development of the poetic, the expressive, in music, as exemplified in the works of Liszt, Wagner, and Berlioz. My symphonic fantasia 'Aus Italien' is the connecting link between the old and the new methods."

Symphonic poems.

That these new methods were indeed those naturally suited to his musical idiosyncrasy Strauss soon found; and he continued to follow them, with ever-increasing mastery, throughout that long series of symphonic poems which forms one of the most important departments of contemporary music. The list is completed by the following titles: Till Eulenspiegel's Merry Pranks and Thus Spake Zarathustra (1894), Don Quixote (1897), A Hero's Life (1898), and the Symphonia Domestica (1903). Since the last date he has devoted himself to operatic composition.* Among his works for the stage are: Feuersnot (1900), Salome (1906), Elektra (1908), and more recently Der Rosencavalier, Ariadne auf Naxos, and The Legend of Joseph.

III

Precedents and innovations.

What were, then, the "new methods" which Strauss began in 1886 to work with? Essentially they were the methods of Berlioz and Liszt, employed with greater skill by a more highly endowed artist. As we saw in the case of Berlioz, the founder of musical realism, this school tries rather to "tell a story" than to "express emotion"; it prefers "brilliancy and vividness" to "depth and poignancy"; it is "objective" rather than "subjective." In the choice of its theme or musical ideas, then, in their development and manipulation, and in its modes of constructing or composing them into complete pieces, it aims first of all at characterization, only secondarily at beauty;

*Strauss has recently brought out (Oct., 1915) an "Alpine Symphony."

CHAP. XIV

and the success of its practitioners is to be determined by their ability to make themes, development, and form thus subserve the interests of characterization.

Vivid portraiture.

In all these matters Strauss excels his forerunners. Probably, on the whole, no composer has ever written such vividly characterized themes. Till Eulenspiegel's chief motive, for instance, only seven notes altogether, is a marvel of delineation of this impertinent, impish rascal, utterly without respect for anything in earth or heaven, perpetually with his tongue in his cheek, yet withal not without something appealing in his perverse humanity. Strauss seems to have caught all this and put it into those seven notes (Figure XVIIIa). Or take the Hero theme from "Ein Heldenleben" (Figure XVIIIb). Here is a good instance of Strauss's indifference to beauty in the pursuit of character. With its old jerks and jumps, its erratic, abrupt discharges of nervous energy, its musically disagreeable intervals (as in that run in sixteenth notes in the third measure), it is as a melody strangely ugly, repellant, almost painful. Yet it paints to the life the self-assertiveness, the pomposity, the vain swagger and brutal egotism of the Hero, who, of course, as Strauss conceives him, is far from a Beethoven hero. As a contrast to these two energetic subjects, we may take the death theme from "Death and Transfiguration." Here is no melody at all, nothing but a rhythm (Figure XVIIIc); yet so unerringly has the composer seized his subject that in this halting,

FIGURE XVIII

(*a*) Till Eulenspiegel theme.

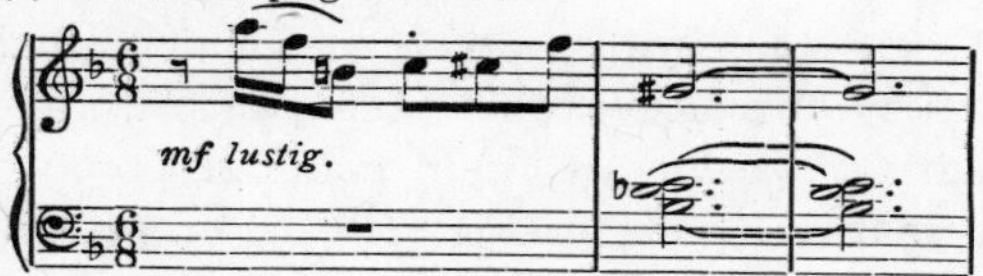

(*b*) "The Hero." Theme from "The Hero's life."

(*c*) Death motive, from "Death and Transfiguration."

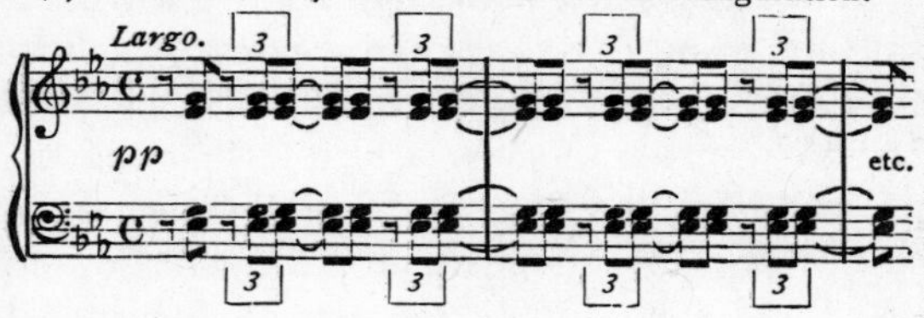

gasping, broken series of notes we hear, as it were, the stertorous breathing of approaching death.

Constructive power.

Greatly as Strauss excels his models in the strongly chiselled profile of his themes, he is equally superior in their manipulation. In this matter his surprising skill in contrapuntal working stands him in good stead; without counterpoint, the interweaving of melodies, there is no real manipulation, and both Berlioz and Liszt were mere tyros compared with Strauss in contrapuntal technique. It is not necessary to take extreme instances like the passage in "A Hero's Life," where he introduces a score or more of themes from his other works; such skill for skill's sake as that smacks more of artifice than of art. But such a passage as the coda of "Death and Transfiguration," from the entrance of the transfiguration motive, is an example of how he can marshal the most varied themes and fragments of themes in a closely knit web of tone, as thrilling to the sense of beauty as it is bewilderingly complex to the examining intelligence. And we shall have other examples when we come to analyze "Till Eulenspiegel."

And mastery in development.

With this skill in manipulation goes naturally a remarkable constructive power. Strauss frankly adopts, in his later works from "Aus Italien" on, the modern principle that the expressive aim and the nature of the themes in each work shall determine the form, and in many cases he adopts the sectional form of

Berlioz's and Liszt's symphonic poems. In other instances he makes use of classic types of structure, as for example the rondo in "Till Eulenspiegel," the theme and variations in "Don Quixote." The important point is that whatever his scheme may be, he treats it with masterly elasticity and solidity. Adverse criticism has much that it can say of Strauss, but the often-heard charge of "formlessness" is a mistake. To deal with free types of structure as he has done requires more mental power, a deeper analytic penetration of the essential psychology of tonal, harmonic, rhythmic, and thematic relationships than to pour all one's ideas into the convenient, but sometimes inappropriate, mold of the sonata-form. Strauss has said that he always has form in mind while composing, and we can readily believe it, since without careful and far-seeing constructive intelligence he could never have reared such colossal yet solidly organized pieces as "Zarathustra" or "Tod und Verklärung."

IV

Later sensationalism.

If we concede to Strauss, however, superiority to his predecessors, Berlioz and Liszt, in vividness of thematic characterization, in contrapuntal manipulation, and in constructive power, we cannot acquit him of having succumbed even more than they to the peculiar temptations of the realistic school. All realism in music, not being held in check by the test of truth to inner feeling as is the more subjective type of art, tends to go to extremes, to pander to public love of sensation, and to lose simplicity and sincerity. We saw the mischievous effects of this tendency in Liszt's pompous swagger and cloying sentimentality, in Berlioz's morbid craving for the horrible and the fantastic. All these traits recur in Strauss. It is notable that his emotion hardly ever has the sincerity and dignity of Beethoven and Schumann; it is always either over-emphatic or a little perfumed. But the pursuit of the sensational is his chief artistic sin. It grew upon him apace from the time he first adopted his later style. We see it in his subjects; in the painful depicting of the death struggle in "Death and Transfiguration"; in the over-pretentious philosophy of "Zarathustra"; in the almost crazy egotism of "The Hero's Life" and the "Symphonia Domestica," obviously autobiographical; and above all in the operas, in the morbid sensuality of "Salome," the mad hate of "Elektra," the cynical voluptuousness of "The Rose Cavalier."

Exaggeration of the "characteristic."

We see it again in much of his later technical procedure. Thus the "characteristic" in melody, the queer turns, jumps, and intervals, is often abused in recent years, so that the melodies lose their musical beauty and become almost epileptically contorted. The skill in counterpoint, too, is abused, as when he fills up his score with line after line of notes that are hardly heard at all, or only thicken and perturb the musical texture. Great as is his mastery of the orchestra, again, a perverse impishness often makes him deny the instruments what they can do best and set them to sniggering and snarling and grunting as if the orchestra were become a menagerie.

What the outcome of this unfortunate sensationalism will be we cannot tell. It may be that Strauss has already done his best work, and that the "Symphonia Domestica," as Mr. Newman, formerly one of his most devoted admirers, suggests, is "the work of an enormously clever man who was once a genius." Or it may be that we do not yet grasp the elements of beauty in his most recent work. Or, still again, it may be that he will himself feel that he has exhausted the possibilities in this direction, and must turn back to a less extreme kind of music. At any rate, he has written enough masterpieces to place himself securely among the greatest of modern composers.

Example for analysis, No. 24. "Till Eulenspiegel's Merry Pranks." After an old Rogue's Tale, in Rondo Form. (An arrangement for piano, two hands, by Otto Singer, is published in the Universal Edition.)

Till Eulenspiegel, or Owlglass, as his name is literally translated in the English version of the story, is the hero of a fifteenth century German *Volksbuch,* a wandering mechanic of Brunswick, who plays all sorts of jokes upon every one, and in spite of his constant flouting of all the respectabilities and decencies, always manages to come out ahead. The German name is said to refer to the old proverb, "Man sees his own faults as little as a monkey or an owl recognizes his ugliness in looking into a mirror."

When the composer was asked, at the time

of the first performance of the work in Cologne, November 5, 1895, to give a clue to his meaning, he replied:

"It is impossible for me to furnish a program to Eulenspiegel; were I to put into words the thoughts which its several incidents suggested to me, they would seldom suffice and might even give rise to offense. Let me leave it, therefore, to my hearers to 'crack the hard nut' which the rogue has provided for them. By way of helping them to a better under-

Figure XIX

standing, it seems sufficient to point out the two Eulenspiegel motives (see Figures XIXa and XIXb) which, in the most manifold disguises, moods and situations, pervade the whole up to the catastrophe, when—after he has been condemned to death—Till is strung up to the gibbet. For the rest, let them guess at the musical joke which a rogue has offered them."

The title states that the work is in rondo form, but it is a rather free type of rondo. The unity and variety of the structure are, however, admirable. The two motives form the basis of everything, but the diversity of their developments is endless. The piece, as a whole, is held together by the similarity of its prologue and its epilogue, and by the exposition (pages 4-6) and recapitulation (pages 19-21) of the chief themes in the ruling tonality of F major.

Prologue or Introduction.—The preliminary suggestion of the opening notes of motive A in moderate tempo (Gemächlich—easy, comfortable) suggests, as Mr. Wilhelm Klatte happily phrases it in his official analysis, the "Once upon a time" of the story-books. It is quickly followed by motive B in the guise of a horn solo, highly effective for the instrument and interesting as showing by its shifting accents the rhythmic ingenuity that characterizes the entire work (Figure XIXc). This is briefly, but brilliantly, developed.

Exposition of Themes.—At the beginning of the fourth line on page 4 Theme A appears for the first time in full—Till makes his bow, or rather his grimace (Figure XIXd). The whimsicality of this is carried out in all this page and the next; at page 5, line 4, the theme returns *fortissimo* in all the woodwind, shrill and impertinent. A variant of Theme B also will be noticed in the fifth line. At the bottom of the page comes a milder form of the main theme, a charming flute solo, followed by delicate imitations. With the cadence in the second line of page 7 the exposition ends. It will be noted that the characteristic motive of two sixteenth notes and an eighth with which Theme A opens dominates it throughout.

Prank I.—Against a persistent tremolo of violas, the basses outline an ingratiating variant of Theme A—Till, innocent and agreeable, almost naïve, winning the confidence he is about to abuse (Figure XIXe). At the bottom of the page comes a rapid upward scale in triplets (clarinets): he jumps upon a horse, and amid the shrill protestation of the market women (woodwind, top of page 8) rides in among their pots and pans. At the height of the turmoil he escapes (trombones in an augmented version of the main motive, bottom of page 8), leaving the women plaintively mourning their broken crockery (minor seconds, pianissimo, page 9).

Prank II.—Gemächlich, B flat major, page 10.

Till masquerades in the costume of a priest, suggested by a simple, pious German folk tune. That he is still the same rascal is suggested by his motive roguishly sounded ("schelmisch") by a small clarinet, at the beginning of the fourth line. The student should also note the variants of the same motive that are dextrously woven into the harmonic tissue, as for example in the bass of line 3 meas. 1-2, in the soprano at line 3, meas. 3-4, and in the alto or tenor at line 4, meas. 2. The curious *una corda* passage for muted horns, trumpets, and solo violins has been said to suggest the hero's discomfort in his untruthful garments, and the chromatic scale (top of page 11) his doffing of them.

Prank III.—Sehr Lebhaft. Till becomes a Don Juan. As he makes love to a village maiden his theme takes on an unmistakably sentimental air, and bits of the second theme sporadically appear in waltz time (bottom of this page). Gradually this theme assumes the upper hand, from the top of page 12, where it appears in the key of G minor, onward. One of the most beautiful bits of part writing in the entire work is that in which it is set against itself, appearing simultaneously in two different rhythms, as shown perhaps rather better in Figure XIXf, than in Singer's arrangement. But, alas! the lady laughs at Till's advances, and he has no refuge for his wounded vanity but in furious anger (bottom of page 12, Theme B inverted, in the bass, and the emphatic augmentations of Theme A, audaciously harmonized, that fill page 13).

Prank IV.—A minor, page 14, line 2.

Till sees a procession of village dignitaries, worthy burghers of philistine respectability, as is suggested by the heavy tread of their theme. He cannot resist making fun of them; fragments of both his themes, in quick nervous rhythms, flash across their stolidity. Their hostility is aroused (all of page 15), and after bearding them outrageously (bottom of page

16) he makes his escape (Leichtfertig, A flat major, 2/4).

Recapitulation.—With page 18 begins a passage in C major, the dominant of the original key, planned to lead back to it, and presenting in new rhythm and novel tonal relations the notes of Theme A (Figure XIXg). From the top of page 19 on, the student will have no difficulty in recognizing for himself divers forms of the main themes, some here recapitulated, others new. At the bottom of page 21 they proceed together, in double harness. A long and gradual climax (pages 22-23) culminates in a brilliant reassertion of the theme of Prank II, in D major (page 24, line 3). But with the sudden diminished seventh chord and ominous drum roll Till's activities cease. He is summoned before an angry jury (F minor chords, bottom of page 24) and tried for his life. His impertinent retorts avail him nothing. He is condemned to death (bold descent of a major seventh, page 25, line 4) and his soul passes (line 4, meas. 6-8).

Epilogue.—The introductory version of the theme recurs, as if to say, "Thus, my children, happened these events in the legendary life of Till Eulenspiegel, long, long ago." In the fourth line on the last page both themes are reduced, so to speak, to their lowest terms, and die away in the sustained chord of A flat. A brief *tutti* ends the piece brilliantly.

CHAPTER XV

Claude Debussy

I

N PASSING from Strauss to Debussy* we pass not only from Germany to France, which is in itself a considerable transition, but from one strongly marked attitude towards art to another which, though equally peculiar to the special epoch in which we live, is sharply contrasted with it, so that the two might be almost called the two poles of the contemporary musical world. The German seeks massiveness, solidity, brilliancy, supersaturated sonorities and overpowering force, multiplying the means to these ends, in his gigantic orchestra, with a prodigality truly barbaric. The Frenchman, on the other hand, prefers suggestion to realization, the creation of an atmosphere to the expression of an emotion, the refined and elusive to the blatant sonority, and in general pursues exclusively those half-shades, those delicate nuances, which only

Early work.

*Claude Achille Debussy was born at St.-Germain-en-Laye, near Paris, in 1862.

a highly civilized, almost effete taste can appreciate. Thus he employs in "Pelléas et Melisande" a comparatively small orchestra, and lets even that produce its full power but infrequently; in his piano pieces as well as in the orchestral sketches and in the charmingly delicate string quartet, his almost constant indication is "pianissimo"; whatever medium he may chance to be using, he seeks to draw from it subtlety rather than fulness or brilliance of color. In short, his artistic quest, like that of his fellow-countryman, Verlaine, is "La nuance, la nuance toujours."

Debussy a subject of controversy.

Naturally enough, so extreme a manifestation of the impressionistic or symbolistic* type of music as this has found enthusiastic disciples and equally earnest detractors, so that Debussy is one of the chief storm-centres of musical controversy, and the student will find the most various and directly contradictory views expressed about him. Thus Mrs. Franz Liebich, in her biography of him in the Living Masters of Music series, writes: "His quick sensibility enables him to seize the most delicate effects of light and shade, and he has rendered his art a plastic medium for recording fleeting impressions and fugitive glimpses." Mr. Paderewski, on the other hand, has expressed his view† frankly and suggestively

*Debussy's art has striking resemblances both with impressionism in painting and with symbolism in literature, to discuss which here would however take us too far afield.

†In "A Conversation on Music," in the Century Magazine, November, 1908.

(whether we agree with him or not) as follows: "Debussy is a man of great skill in harmony and orchestration, but he writes music not for its own sake, but as handmaid to something that is not music. Now music is not a handmaid, a slave; it should not be made subordinate to poetry, a mere decoration; it should have its own form, its own meaning, its own *raison d'être*. Not long ago I heard 'Pelléas et Melisande' in Paris. It is ingenious, it has many beautiful effects, but from beginning to end it is subdued, soft, monotonous—everything is subordinated to the text, nothing is musically salient—pages and pages without one common chord and without rhythmic vigor—never one manly accent." To such criticisms as this Debussy's admirers are apt to retort with Mrs. Liebich, not, it will be noticed, without a rather unfair resort to epithets, such as "strong" and "violent," which beg the question at issue: "Those addicted to strong colors and violent contrasts, and indifferent to delicate subtle suggestion, refinement, and spirituality, will have no affinity with M. Debussy's typical, original harmonies, fluid rhythm, free chord combinations, and elastic, flowing melodies."

Because of his attitude toward music.

Such differences of opinion are hardly to be bridged, because they rest ultimately on profound differences of temperament and instinctive taste regarding which argument is proverbially vain. They may, however, be to some extent understood if we can only get clearly in mind the peculiarity of Debussy's attitude that is described by Mr. Paderewski's phrase, "Everything is subordinated to the text, nothing is musically salient." Debussy in fact writes music not for its own sake, not to produce a purely musical beauty and expression, as does, for example, Schumann, on which the listener's mind is to be concentrated, but to suggest an atmosphere or mood, to carry the mind away from the sounds to something they may vaguely symbolize, to afford a background for the kind of day-dreaming that so many people imagine to be the end and aim of music. If we examine his most characteristic methods with this conception of his purpose in mind, we shall find that they are all accounted for by it, and that he is literally, as he is often fancifully called, a painter of tone-pictures, a suggester of moods, rather than a maker of music.

II

Symbolistic methods.

First of all, in his choice of subjects and titles he reveals a preference for the vague, the mystical, the elusive, as best suited to evoke at once that state of reverie or day-dreaming in the listener, that preoccupation with his own moods rather than with objective beauty in the work of art, at which symbolism aims. The Pre-Raphaelesque "Blessed Damosel," to Rossetti's text, had early shown his natural leaning toward mystical subjects; but it was not until after he had received the impetus of close association with impressionistic painters, poets, and literary critics at the house of the

Chap. XV

symbolist poet Stéphane Mallarmé that he consciously embraced these tendencies, as exemplified in his famous orchestral prelude to Mallarmé's "The Afternoon of a Faun" (1892). As for the "Pelléas et Melisande" of Maeterlinck, the text of his famous opera, at which he was at work from 1892 to 1902, its symbolism and mysticism are too familiar to require any comment. The orchestral "Nocturnes" (1899) bear such sub-titles as "Clouds" and "Festivals," and the later "La Mer" (1905) is divided into "From Dawn to Noon on the Sea"; "Play of the Surges"; and "Dialogue of the Wind and Sea." Turning to the piano pieces, we find such names as "Moonlight," "Gardens in the Rain," "Pagodas," "Reflections in the Water," "Gold Fish," "Bells Through the Leaves" (Cloches à travers les feuilles").

Prefers indefinite to definite effects.

Of course, too much should not be argued from mere titles. These titles are mentioned only as showing a general tendency to help the listener away from the music itself to more or less vague trains of thought, feeling, or picture that it may suggest. It is only when we come to such intrinsic matters as melody and harmony that we can be sure of the tendencies which these names and subjects seem to indicate. And on the whole, Debussy's ways of treating melody and harmony seem to bear out our theory: that is, they seem calculated to reduce the purely musical interest to a minimum, by veiling or disguising all definite musical traits, and to enhance the sensuous charm of the tonal combinations at the expense of their intellectual and even their emotional interest, in order the better to stimulate or seduce the hearer into a half hypnotic state of reverie. This minimizing of the intellectual element, together with the enhancement of the purely sensuous charm which it aids, is traceable in almost every element of Debussy's musical technique.

Both in melody.

In melody, for example, the intellectual and emotional appeal depends in large measure on the variety, breadth, and rhythmic diversity in unity of the melodic line or curve. In listening to such a melody as the Prize Song in Wagner's "Die Meistersinger," for instance, we follow attentively and with delight each phrase as it unfolds itself, feeling the interesting variety that it contributes to the tune, the balance it sets up with other phrases, and all the time holding fast our sense of the unity of the whole complex series of tones and phrases. Speaking technically, such a tune requires many subtle contrasts in the lengths and accents of the notes used, and in the choice of resting places or cadences employed: it is a highly complex unity, which only a master can create and only an attentive listener can grasp. Now Debussy carefully avoids all such melody. He works rather with brief fragments of which the notes are often all alike or nearly alike in value—fragments that will not make any demands on the hearer's attention. "Jardins sous la pluie," for instance, is built up on the bit of melody announced by

CHAP. XV

the left hand, in even notes, in the first two measures.* Moreover, he studiously evades those cadences which in most music serve as breathing places where the listener may pause before renewing his attention, or as punctuation marks to make clear the structure of the musical sentence. Debussy is curiously cadenceless. The reason is that he is writing not sentences, definite statements, but collocations of suggestive words.

And in harmony.

But it is in harmony that his methods reveal their motives most clearly, and obtain their most striking results. Here, again, the principle seems to be subordination of musical significance to sensuous charm. This may best be demonstrated by illustration.

Example for analysis, No. 25. "La Soirée dans Grenade," from "Estampes."

The first two pages are introductory. Over a pedal point on low C sharp, the incisive rhythm of the habanera, a well-known Spanish dance, is suggested. A fragment of folk-melody, characterized by the peculiar scale interval of the sharpened fourth-step (B sharp in this case), which we discussed in connection with Grieg, is sketched in softly by the left hand, under the persistent pedal point of C sharp, now placed in the very high register (measures 7-16). This passage is of a peculiar and most original sonority. With the *Tempo giusto* comes a bit of such thoroughly Debussyan harmony that if we can fully un-

*The point will be made quite clear by a comparison of this bit with the "second theme," on page 20, which is much more of a melody, though not of great (musical) interest.

derstand these four measures we shall be in possession of the key to the peculiar style which he represents.

The chord here employed in a most individual way is in itself one of the commonest we have—the so-called "dominant-seventh chord." It is what is called a dissonant chord; that is, it contains tones which grate against each other, and which the ear naturally wishes to have move into tones which harmonize—a process technically known as "resolution." Originally all dissonant chords could be tolerated only if their tones did thus resolve in an orderly and well-understood way, for which there were definite rules, and also if they were introduced with equal care by what was called "preparation." Monteverde (1567-1643) is, as a matter of fact, credited with being the first composer to use this very "dominant-seventh chord" without such careful preparation. To put the same thing in a slightly different way, all chords, or momentary combinations of tone, were originally but secondary results of the movement of a number of melodies going on at once; and it was quite natural that when a chord thus produced was dissonant or harsh, composers should at first feel that it was justified only if the motions of the melodies which produced it were carefully guided and made plain to the ear. All the complicated rules of "preparation" and "resolution" were simply formulations of these necessary motions of the melodies which originally created the dissonant chords in question, also often called "dependent" because they referred forward to the more consonant chord of resolution.

Gradually, however, the melodic origin of such chords was forgotten, their familiarity made them acceptable to the ear in spite of and even because of their dissonance (since dissonance lends richness and "spiciness"), and they were treated more and more as "independent," capable of any and every sort of connection. Now Debussy, in a passage like the present one, simply carries to an extreme this ignoring of the melodic meaning of a chord in order to take advantage of its sensuous richness. He writes a whole series of dominant-seventh chords without reference to the resolution of their dissonant tones. It would be pedantic to object to such a procedure; it is quite legitimate as a means to a particular end—a certain kind of sonority; all that criticism should do is to point out that the chords are not here being used as derivatives of melodies going on at once, but as *blocks of tone, supporting a single melody.* Debussy's musical imagination is essentially homophonic ("one-melodied"): just as we saw that he makes his single melodies as brief and musically primitive as possible, so he instinctively makes his harmony in blocks supporting the single melody, instead of weaving it out of coöperating melodies as composers more bent on music and less on sensuous charm usually do.

Returning to the analysis, we find at the

top of page 10 another intensely characteristic passage of six measures illustrating another mode of carrying out the same tendencies. Here is the famous Debussyan "whole-tone scale," a scale which is not, by the way, peculiar to Debussy, although he has probably done more than any other man to exploit its possibilities and to make it an accepted and valued part of the modern musical idiom.

The whole-tone scale differs from all other scales, except the "chromatic," in that all its intervals are precisely equal—it consists of seven tones, each separated from its neighbor by the interval of a "whole tone" or "major second." The scale Debussy is using here, for example, is shown in Figure XX. The re-

Figure XX

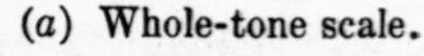

(*a*) **Whole-tone scale.**

(*b*) **Passage from "La Soirée dans Grenade," based on this scale.**

sult of this equality of interval, on which depends the charm of this scale as a contrast with the ordinary diatonic scales, is that it abolishes completely the sense of tonality or key. A series of chords based on the ordinary scales give a sense of direction, of relation to a definite center or point of rest (the "keynote"), which may be compared with our sense of direction in ordinary life, based on a knowledge of the points of the compass. In listening to it we "know," as we say, "where we are." But the whole-tone scale is agreeably bewildering: it has no tonal up or down, left or right, east, west, north, or south. It reminds one of the Irishman's feeling about the ocean; he preferred a railroad accident to a collision at sea: "for," said he, "if you are wrecked on land there you are, but if you are wrecked at sea where are you?" The lack of definiteness in the whole-tone scale, of course, has the effect, like other veilings of musical form, of concentrating our attention on the sensuous charm of the material, which moreover is intrinsically great because the harmonies appropriate to it are rich and still comparatively unfamiliar.*

The passage in dominant sevenths now returns, followed by one in which "common chords" or "triads" are similarly used; and

*This is too technical a point to go into here. As the harmony student knows, neither the "common chord" nor the "dominant seventh" can be used with the whole-tone scale, which requires rather "augmented triads" and dominant sevenths with "altered tones."

with the "Très rhythmé" the main theme enters in A major—a vigorous dance-tune in which dislocations of accent similar to our American rag-time will be noticed. A passage somewhat similar to that in the whole-tone scale occurs in the second line on page 12. Here "triads" are used as harmonic blocks supporting a single melody, in the manner described above.

The same procedure, exceedingly quaint in effect, is better illustrated in the "Léger et lointain" ("Light and distant") on page 13. We are reminded of guitars being plucked in the distance, almost out of ear-shot. The effect is highly poetic. The piece ends softly with a return of the introductory melody.

If the student will examine carefully almost any piano piece of Debussy's he will find examples of these two characteristic harmonic processes—the use of chords as "blocks" without reference to the melodic quality of their constituent tones, and the use of whole-tone scale harmony. In "Jardins sous la pluie," for instance, the first is illustrated in the curious "scherzando" at the bottom of page 23, and the second through the measures following the double bar on page 18.

III

Summary.

Debussy has undoubtedly contributed invaluable elements to the modern musical vocabulary. Not only is his feeling for all the delicate and elusive sonorities of the piano so keen that it would hardly be an exaggeration to say that he has elicited more new effects from the keyboard than any composer since Chopin, but in the more fundamental matter of harmonic idiom he has made a real contribution in his treatment of already familiar materials and especially in his exploitation of the whole-tone scale. Although the slightness of his musical thought reduces the intellectual and emotional appeal of his music, and makes it wear not very well, no composer, in an age given to delicate trifling and the search for new sensations, has achieved a more subtle charm, a more varied palette of halftones and delicious tonal nuances, than he.